AF674424

IRRATIONALLY PASSIONATE

Praise for *Irrationally Passionate*

'One of the most riveting, raw, authentic and insightful stories of an entrepreneur I have ever come across. An epic turnaround journey that is a must-read for young readers.'

– **Karan Johar**

'I have known Jason for some time and have always been impressed with his drive, clarity and vision. This biography has helped me appreciate him even more. From the time he handles a tough negotiation for a chess set as a child, to his turnaround brilliance in the corporate world, there is a lot that entrepreneurs can learn from him; not just bookish, theoretical knowledge, but actual real-life lessons learnt from the School of Hard Knocks. This book is a must-read if you are an entrepreneur!'

– **Amish Tripathi**, best-selling author of *The Shiva Trilogy*

'Living and surviving across continents, embracing and seeking challenges, and finding enormous courage in difficult situations, Jason has an inspiring story which needs to be told. A self-made entrepreneur, he recounts the many risks and learnings that will strike a note with seasoned founders and promoters as well as the new-age tech whiz kids. Thoroughly engaging, anecdotal and without a moment of ennui ... this one comes straight from the heart and says it as it is!'

– **Priti Rathi Gupta**, MD, Anand Rathi

'A very engaging, hard-hitting yet emotionally bound narrative of a rebel turned enviable entrepreneur. Thought-provoking depiction of what one makes of the advantages and challenges life throws at you whilst relishing the highs, surviving the lows, fighting the anguish and through it all superbly carving a niche for oneself. A delightfully interesting and fascinating read, which has made me respect Jason even more for his fighting spirit, grit, confidence and determination.'

– **Anuj Puri**, Chairman, Anarock Property Consultants

'I have had the privilege to work closely with Jason in multiple turnaround situations. Jason's calmness, clarity, candour and co-ordination helps him effectively navigate through the stormiest of situations. Any company in crisis should have Jason on speed dial.'

– **Suvir Sujan**, Co-founder, Nexus Venture Partners;
Board Director, Housing.com and Snapdeal

'The way to make a small fortune in entertainment is to start with a large one. The business of making comics and turning them into TV shows, motion pictures and merchandise is challenging and complex. Jason, at Valiant Entertainment, was exceptional. His success in reviving Valiant from the ashes is a rare and admirable feat. Jason is a very sharp, dynamic, relentless yet balanced entrepreneurial leader with a wonderful sense of humour and humility who maintains good cheer even through the most trying of times.'

– **Bill Jemas**, former COO, Marvel Entertainment

'To believe you can, to educate yourself to be able and to find the doors and, if necessary, the windows and make it happen. Jason walks the walk and learnt a long time ago, there is no box to think out of. To create and invent is divine, but to implement is what it really is about. Jason knows.'

– **Peter Dekom**, former Partner, Bloom, Dekom &
Hergott, named by *Premiere* magazine as one of
the 50 *Most Powerful People in Hollywood*

IRRATIONALLY PASSIONATE

My Turnaround from Rebel to Entrepreneur

JASON KOTHARI

18 17

HARPER
BUSINESS

An Imprint of HarperCollins *Publishers*

First published in India in 2020 by Harper Business
An imprint of HarperCollins *Publishers*
A-75, Sector 57, Noida, Uttar Pradesh 201301, India
www.harpercollins.co.in

2 4 6 8 10 9 7 5 3 1

Copyright © Jason Kothari 2020

P-ISBN: 978-93-5357-265-5
E-ISBN: 978-93-5357-266-2

The views and opinions expressed in this book are the author's own and the facts are as reported by him, and the publishers are not in any way liable for the same.

Jason Kothari asserts the moral right to be identified as the author of this work.

All rights reserved. No part of this publication may be reproduced, stored in a retrieval system, or transmitted, in any form or by any means, electronic, mechanical, photocopying, recording or otherwise, without the prior permission of the publishers.

Typeset in 11/15 Minion Pro at
Manipal Technologies Limited, Manipal

Printed and bound at
Thomson Press (India) Ltd

MIX
Paper
FSC FSC® C010615

This book is produced from independently certified FSC® paper to ensure responsible forest management.

To all the entrepreneurs who work so hard and sacrifice so much to try and change their life, their family's lives and the world around them. I salute every one of you.

To my parents who are the finest human beings I have ever known. Everything is for you.

Contents

Author's Note

MANY ENTREPRENEURS GOING through very difficult situations or trying to see beyond the horizon approach me. They're usually seeking advice on critical decisions or even sometimes just seeking a kindred spirit who can understand what they're going through. I always make it a point to meet them. During some of the most trying times in my career, I have had the good fortune of finding advisors and mentors, possibly salvaging years of my life, so it's something I'm passionate about doing for others who think they can benefit from my experiences.

I have advised a wide spectrum of entrepreneurs, from students with just an idea to founders of large established companies, but I find the interactions fulfilling no matter what the stage is. Often the discussion involves providing a different perspective backed up by personal examples from my own collection of "war" stories, which not only helps convey the point more clearly but also builds mutual trust between the entrepreneur and me, making our bond stronger and our conversations more enriching.

On one of these occasions, a young entrepreneur said I should write a book. I literally laughed it off. She repeated this suggestion, and I laughed it off again. She politely nudged me to take her suggestion seriously, as my advice may have changed the trajectory of her business and life, and, as a former publishing executive, she believed that a book would be the right medium to reach many more entrepreneurs like her. I agreed to consider it but was still not convinced.

Based on her behest, I met HarperCollins, my eventual publisher. They understood I would only invest the several hundreds of hours required to create a book if I felt I could offer something uniquely valuable to readers, many of whom are already exposed to plenty of material on entrepreneurship and business leadership. We asked some key questions—what kind of book would be most helpful to young entrepreneurs in India today? Does it already exist? We talked to many young entrepreneurs, as well as their families and friends, and realized that a truly open and honest story of an entrepreneur's journey—one that discussed the personal, professional, failures and successes, and connected all these dots to give a complete and accurate picture—is something they need more than ever. However, being a naturally private and reserved person, I completely rejected the idea at first.

Later, upon reflection, I realized that if I was serious about giving back to other entrepreneurs earlier in their journey, this is the most valuable thing I could do for them. Perhaps it would also inspire other entrepreneurs to do the same, making them realize sharing their story authentically and openly, even the uncomfortable parts, is possibly the most important thing they can do for fellow entrepreneurs and future generations of business leaders. But it isn't easy, and it certainly wasn't easy for me.

Irrationally passionate is something all entrepreneurs are – the risk / return profile of entrepreneurship never justifies becoming an entrepreneur. Furthermore, being a turnaround business leader that rebuilds companies in crisis is even zanier. But few things can be more intensely satisfying, and I'm proud to be part of this irrationally passionate tribe that pushes the status quo and tackles outsized challenges. This book in itself is an example of that. You will see.

I hope you enjoy it, it helps you in your journey, and it also encourages you to share your story one day. I would be happy to hear from you at Jason@irrationally-passionate.com. All my author's proceeds will be donated to the charitable trust that supports Shri Sai Baba's Temple in Shirdi.

Prologue

MY EARLIEST BRUSH with entrepreneurship occurred on the sun-baked streets of Agra on the way to the Taj Mahal with my parents. I was eight years old. As we walked, street vendors hawked their wares, barking out bargains to anyone who would listen. My eyes darted towards a large shiny chess set sitting on a market table. I stopped walking.

'I want that,' I said, tugging my father's arm.

'That chessboard? Okay. Well, you have your own money,' he said. 'Go make him an offer.'

I stepped up to the stern looking forty-something street vendor nervously, and cleared my throat.

'How much does this chess set cost?' I almost whispered.

'Five hundred rupees,' came the reply.

I ran my small fingers over a rook and a bishop before lifting the queen off the board, turning it over in my hand. I looked up at my father. He nodded, a signal to let the negotiations commence. My Gujarati business credibility hung in the balance.

'Thirty rupees,' I told the seller confidently.

'Thirty rupees?' he howled, 'This is a solid marble set, the pieces are hand-carved! Four-hundred rupees.'

His dismissive tone was intended to shame me for having the audacity to bargain. But it didn't. It stirred my competitive juices. The discount wasn't enough. I wanted more.

'I think the price should be thirty rupees,' I said loudly.

'Too low!' the man replied with a chuckle. 'I can't go that low. I will give it to you for two hundred and fifty rupees.'

He was bluffing and I knew it.

I looked up at my father. His narrowed gaze screamed 'stand strong'.

I had already shaved a lot off the original price and felt proud for having done so. But like so much else later in my life, that day I wanted to push things to the extreme. I looked back up at the vendor.

'Thirty rupees,' I said smiling.

Apparently no one had yet taught me that price negotiation involves a buyer and seller meeting somewhere in the middle. So instead, I just kept holding firm to my opening offer. And with each exchange, the man's price kept falling.

Back and forth we haggled. At somewhere around the ₹125 mark, the vendor shot my mother an exasperated look. She just shrugged. 'Don't look at me,' her body language said. 'We have to *live* with the boy.'

Finally, after ten minutes, whether out of sheer exhaustion or frustration, the vendor relented.

'Fine,' he said with a huff. 'Thirty rupees.'

In my mind I can still see my father's face, beaming with pride. The rest of the day I carried my new chessboard like a trophy.

'You didn't let up!' my father said with a smile over lunch. 'I'm proud of you. Very proud.'

I still remember those words. It is one of the few times he has ever praised me. My father came from the old school. A proud Rajkot native, he was brought up with the belief that too many compliments might spoil a child and stifle a humble spirit. So compliments and praise were a rare occurrence.

Today that chessboard sits in my parents' home. When my father feels a pang of nostalgia, he brings it up as a proxy for telegraphing his pride.

'Remember the chessboard?' he says with a grin.

Since that day in Agra I've been fortunate enough to negotiate dozens of deals totalling billions of dollars. But that first negotiation still holds a special place in my heart. It was the first of many steps along an entrepreneurial journey that transformed the trajectory of my life.

No entrepreneur's path is ever a straight line. Setbacks are constant, disappointments guaranteed. Moreover, no one is born an entrepreneur; they are forged in the rough and tumble crucible of life. It's not for everyone. But in my years in business, I have learned that few things are as fulfilling professionally as turning an idea into reality, creating meaningful jobs for others, working tirelessly with teammates to overcome obstacles, and serving customers with an impactful product or service.

The key, I believe, is mastering the art of the turnaround. Not just in business but in life as well. With all due respect to my professors at Wharton, learning how to orchestrate a comeback can't be learned solely in a classroom studying business theory. And triggering a turnaround in one's personal life is even harder. But it can be done with the power of passion.

Today when I'm asked to give talks on entrepreneurship, audiences often ask me questions based on a news article they've read about me or a company I've helped turn around. But the media accounts are often incomplete or sometimes even inaccurate; the true story is more complex and gritty. Messy even.

When business people describe me today as a 'turnaround man', they don't know the half of it. Beyond stopping a company's freefall or helping to send its revenues or profits climbing, some of my biggest turnarounds were personal. Growing up in countries around the world, an Indian outsider with a funny name, I learnt to confront bigotry. I turned around my grades, from being a decent student to becoming a top student; turned things right side up after my first true love was stricken with cancer, turning my world upside down; rediscovering my Jain roots helped me kick smoking and excessive drinking when I swerved off course in college. A 'turnaround man', indeed.

I'm not proud of every decision I've made in my life. But entrepreneurship driven by passion forced me to become a better person. It made me evolve, grow, and demand more from myself. I believe this, and not the monetary rewards, was the greatest value I gained from entrepreneurship.

In this book I will share what I've learned along the way—all of it, the ugly and the beautiful. My hope for you is that my experiences will serve you in your life's journey. If you're a parent, the stories I will recount will give you greater insight into the exciting opportunities your child can seize, particularly in our country's nascent entrepreneurial ecosystem. If you're a young dreamer like I was, I hope this book will offer you valuable tools and lessons that will cut years off your learning curve, allowing you to fly as high as your wings will carry you.

Most of all, in your life and business, I want to demonstrate to you of one of life's most axial truths—irrational passion is the fuel that empowers us to achieve beyond what we think is possible—and it taught me that it's never too late for a turnaround.

1

Be True to Your Roots, Embrace Your Passion

BLOOD GUSHED FROM my left nostril. Gauging from the size of the crimson splats on the floor, I was losing the fight and was in trouble. The American boy standing in front of me was six inches taller, at least thirty pounds heavier, and had a crushing right hook.

'Come on, Punjab!' he yelled, while circling me.

My fifteen-year-old fists were clenched, my knuckles red.

I lunged towards him and threw a right uppercut, slicing nothing but air.

'Let's go, Indian!' he taunted.

From the corners of my swelling eyes I could see the hazy silhouettes of three of his friends standing nearby. I hoped they wouldn't join in the beating.

He landed two jabs to my face before torqueing his body like a wrench and slamming another right hook into my ribs.

Why does he hate me? I thought. *Why am I fighting? Why did my parents send me to this godforsaken American boarding school?*

I squared him up and threw a flurry of punches at his torso. I was finally connecting, landing solid blows. He hugged me to stop my flailing arms.

Seconds later the door flung open. A school master barged in.

'Stop it! Right now!' he yelled.

I wiped my nose across my sleeve and wondered if the red smear would come out when washed.

The bully and I were then marched into the administrator's office. They asked all the wrong questions.

'Who started the fight? Do you need to see a doctor? Are either of you here on scholarship?'

I knew anything I said might later be used against me or lead to further teasing from classmates, so I spoke as little as possible. I certainly didn't divulge the truth.

The weeks leading up to the fight had been filled with racial epithets, an unending stream of anti-Indian trash talking about a country the boy knew nothing about. In a futile effort to make peace, I'd loaned him some money. The night of the fight I'd made the mistake of asking him to pay me back. That's when he socked me in the face—something he'd done several times before. Only this time, instead of turning the other cheek, I'd finally had enough. I was done being his punching bag. I fought back.

A native of Brooklyn, New York, my bully had arrived at The Lawrenceville School in New Jersey on scholarship. Looking back now, I realize his tough-guy persona was all an act. Today I feel sympathy for him and forgive him. His bravado was more insecurity than animus. He felt he was admitted to the school more for his athletic skills than anything else. When self-doubt crept in, he lashed out at the nearest and easiest target: me, the Indian kid, the outsider.

I had arrived at the American boarding school because my parents had seen a glossy brochure that promised a world-class education. The fact that it was located not far from Princeton University added to its initial allure. Strangely enough, however, the advert failed to mention the school's reputation for gladiator-style brawls. Local residents in the area nicknamed The Lawrenceville School 'L-ville'. We called it 'Hell-ville'.

Sadly, my one year at Hell-ville would not be the last time I would be forced to fight or be picked on for being Indian. But if the experience taught me anything, it was to stand up for myself and my heritage. More specifically, it taught me to defend my values and be proud of my roots. A teachable moment for life and entrepreneurship, indeed.

Let me start from the beginning.

I was born two months premature, at home, in the congested urban area known as Tsim Sha Tsui in southern Kowloon, Hong Kong, during one of the city's worst typhoons. We lived in an apartment inside a big brown angular building called New World that also housed a shopping mall. New World sat on the water's edge on Kowloon Bay. At night, hundreds of soaring skyscrapers lit up the skyline with a million shimmering lights glinting against the darkness. To visitors and tourists viewing the impressive kaleidoscope of colour from a distance, Hong Kong appeared enchanting, electric, and alive with possibilities. Locals familiar with its seedier underbelly, however, saw it somewhat differently.

Inside our New World apartment there were four of us. My mother Kiran was a highly-educated teacher from Aden, Yemen, whose father hailed from Rajkot. My father Ashok, also a Rajkot native, was a senior executive at a multinational company (MNC). My brother Neil, two years my elder, was the perfect child if ever there was one. Or, to put it another way, the rebellious screw-ups of my youth were not for the lack of a great role model. That's all on me.

When people ask me whether entrepreneurship is innate or learned, I never hesitate to pick the latter. Like most people, I had no upper echelon connections, no millionaire mentor, no inside C-suite executive track. I doubt I even knew what the word 'entrepreneur' meant until my middle teens.

My childhood was nomadic, to say the least. Our family lived wherever my father's work took us. That meant mother, Neil and I bounced from place to place. Hong Kong was more or less our home base, but we spent intermittent bursts of time in different parts of the world as my father's work required. All the zigging and zagging around the globe made forming and maintaining friendships hard enough. Cultural and language barriers (my parents spoke only English and Gujarati in our home) exacerbated the already strong sense of dislocation and loneliness.

Home life wasn't always easy. As children, Neil and I knew we were loved, and we felt lucky to have such kind and caring parents. But my parents' personalities gave them an emotional distance that was sometimes hard to connect with. My father was very patient and understanding, but his formal demeanour and difficulty in recognizing achievements often kept us grasping for his approval. Mom was very affectionate, selfless and a lovely homemaker, but she possessed a temper that sometimes kept us on edge. As Indian expats living in foreign lands, there was no extended family around. And the fact that my parents gave my brother and me odd names only added to our sense of rootlessness.

After completing kindergarten and the first grade in Hong Kong my parents moved us to Pittsburgh, Pennsylvania, where I attended second grade. It was an alien world to me. Everyone was a white American. It also snowed there, something I'd never seen before. On the first day of school, a kid asked me where I was from. 'I'm Indian, but I'm from Hong Kong,' I said. 'Huh?' he replied. 'You're King Kong?'

From then on, I was anxious, always on guard. I tried to fade into the corners of life. Once, a neighbour invited me to a party. I spent nearly the entire time washing dishes and helping in the kitchen. No one forced me to. But at that innocent age, I had already developed a tenderness of spirit that sensed I was inferior, unequal. I thought it was my 'place' to be the 'help'. That feeling manifested itself in an abundance of caution and a painful level of subservience and politeness.

The following year my father moved us to Paris. There I attended third grade. Things got dark quickly. Racism against Indians was overt. There were no illusions about our second-class status. Stores were less than eager to serve you. I was made to sit in a different part of the school bus. The fact that I didn't speak French didn't help either. One day at school, a random boy walked straight up to me and punched me in the stomach as hard as he could. I went unconscious. I was seven years old.

Everyone experiences difficulties during childhood. Neil and I were always blessed with a roof over our heads, food in our stomachs, and the comforts of an upper middle-class upbringing. But I'm not sure my parents could relate to the anxieties our perennial outsider status created. Their general sentiment seemed to be, *figure it out on your own*. Maybe it was their way of conditioning us, toughening us up. I can't say for sure but, regardless, I thank them for it. Because what I do know is that being thrust into unfamiliar and sometimes hostile cultures, like the Paris experience, helped steel me for when I later entered chaotic corporate cultures in need of a turnaround. *Vive la France!*

After a year in Paris, our family returned to Hong Kong where I remained from the age of eight until I was fifteen. During those years we spent several summers in India visiting my father's family in Rajkot and my mother's family in Mumbai. It was on those visits that I felt most at home and alive—a piercing ray of sunshine amid an otherwise unusual childhood.

My grandparents' place in Rajkot was a tiny two-bedroom home. Yet there was always a feeling like we were living this grand life there, one filled with the quality family time I craved (and still do). Whatever we wanted to eat, we ate. Wherever we wanted to go, we went. And we did it together, as a family.

Many mornings grandfather took my brother and me down the road to pick up freshly fried *gathiya*, wrapped in newspaper, with a side of green chillies. We would bring it home, open it up, and share. On special occasions we'd have *jalebi* and play board games while sipping grandmother's masala chai. The home's cramped quarters made the feeling of togetherness all the more strong. I loved it.

The most 'stressful' part of the day was deciding the lunch menu. A vegetarian family, we debated the daily menu and waited for grandfather to come home for lunch, after which he would take a nap and then head back to finish his workday. At a learning centre down the road, I took classes in subjects like typing (not my favourite) and Gujarati. It may sound silly, but I remember feeling proud to learn the language of my homeland. Most school subjects felt burdensome, but not my Gujarati lessons.

Looking back now I realize it was my childlike way of reaching for an ephemeral sense of national identity and belonging, a way of reinforcing my pride in what it means to be Indian. Today, when I hear others speak ill of our nation, I get angry. You'll never know how fortunate you are to live in India, until you've been made to live elsewhere.

At night my grandparents told us stories about our parents, our great-grandparents, and national heroes. There was laughter and affection, love and warmth. It was a beautiful life. At every other period of my life, I was a kid without a country. But not there, not in Rajkot. I felt safe, loved, and like I belonged. I never wanted those summers to end.

But they did.

Soon, it was back to the loud, clogged, and often rough streets of Hong Kong. I did my best to fit in.

Basketball was among the more popular sports at the international school I attended. At first, I hated basketball because I sucked at it. Classmates didn't want me on their team during pick-up games. And who could blame them? I was terrible. But instead of being repelled by the sport, I was drawn to it. Frustration over my poor skills fuelled a determination to improve. That turnaround trait—running towards, not away, from personal weaknesses—became a habit I cultivated and later pushed to extremes in life and business.

Throughout my adolescence and into my early teenage years, basketball became an all-consuming passion. Every day after school I would spend hours practising alone. I would imagine my basketball idol, Michael Jordan, and me playing one-on-one. Month after month I saw my performance improve. Foul shots, three-pointers, layups, hook shots—I drained bucket after bucket. When I beat every opponent in one-on-one pick-up games, I started challenging two guys to play me at once. When I blew through those competitors, I challenged myself to win with an increasing margin and once led a team to a 40-0 victory! It got to the point that I was embarrassed at how dominant I could be. Occasionally I would miss a shot on purpose, just to keep things competitive.

With these skills, I was naturally on all the basketball teams, sometimes captaining them, and won many tournaments. I loved the feeling of being part of something bigger than myself. I also absorbed lessons about leadership and teamwork. I learned the value of building a team of players with strengths that complemented each other, not just putting the best individual players together. Functioning as a unit made me realize the importance of being a selfless player and putting the team first. Sometimes I would get the ball behind the three-point line and have a clear shot on goal. But then I would spot a teammate wide open, closer to the goal, and pass the ball to increase our odds of scoring. Simple lessons, to be sure. But they made a strong impression even then.

Basketball helped me shake some of my awkwardness. But cultural tensions always hovered in the background. A few Indian kids attended my school but most were Chinese and British. So when the usual adolescent dramas arose, classmates would call us '*bhangis*'. In the Indian caste system, the *bhangis* have been a sweeper caste—known for cleaning toilets.

The attitude was, 'Oh, you're Indian? You're probably a toilet cleaner.' Another favourite put down was 'he's Indian—as in the dot, not the feather'. This was, for some, a crass way of delineating between those of us from Asia (a *bindi* on the forehead) versus Native American Indians (those with a feather, as in a headdress). Basketball could only cure so much.

Over time, I began to realize that the sport, while a fun distraction, wasn't going to do much for my life. Considering I was an Indian living in Hong Kong, the likelihood of me ever doing much with basketball beyond high school seemed next to nil. All the time on the court certainly wasn't helping my studies either. My grades were okay, but they were nothing compared to Neil's. He aced everything, was a talented tennis player, and earned straight A's all the way up to high-school graduation before going to Stanford University. As was his way, my brother did his best to help his struggling younger sibling.

'Don't worry, Jason,' Neil would tell me encouragingly. 'Don't compare yourself to me or anyone else. Everyone is different. You have many great qualities I don't have, and you will find your own path and passion. It just takes time. Be patient. Your day will come.'

Prophetic words.

My school in Hong Kong, which was called Island School, encouraged students to get involved in extracurricular activities that promoted volunteer work and charities. Beyond looking good on a resumé, community service work taught us valuable lessons about helping others. So, at age twelve, I was excited when I was named the co-head of charity events for my class. I decided to combine my love of pizza with charity by selling slices of pizza to students who were sick of our school's bland lunch options. One of the most popular pizza brands in Hong Kong was Domino's. Every Tuesday they had a special offer where you could buy one pizza and get another free. And that's when I had a spark of entrepreneurial inspiration.

I took an informal poll to figure out which pizza combinations were most desired and popular, to ensure we bought the right inventory to minimize waste. Next, I marketed the pizza sale the day before by plastering posters all around school to build excitement and demand. I knew the location of the pizza sales would be key, so I staked out prime spots like the playground and near the staff room and enlisted friends to volunteer to work the sales tables on pizza day. I needed people I could trust to manage the sales, who wouldn't eat the pizza or give it away. I then planned to be the runner, going between selling locations, to monitor operations and rearrange inventory based on sales velocity at each location to maximize sales.

The goal was raising money for charity; I needed the economics to work in our favour. Given that our school's cafeteria food wasn't that great—and that my classmates loved Domino's—I knew we could price pizza slices at a premium. I ordered thirty pizzas. Each had eight slices. After the buy-one-get-one-free offer, the purchase cost per pizza worked out to $3. I set the price per slice at $1. As it turned out, we sold 29 pizzas and only had one unsold. The final math: $232 revenue minus $87 (cost of goods sold minus $3 for the unsold pizza) equalled to $142 in profit in a single hour.

I couldn't believe it. Whether I fully realized it then or not, I'd devised a business plan and it worked! Not only did we donate the full amount to charity, we were also informed that we had raised one of the highest amounts by a student-organized charity in our school. It was such a smash hit that I was eager to run the pizza charity sale every Tuesday to leverage the Domino's buy-one-get-one-free opportunity, but school administrators told me that was too aggressive. (Thanks for stifling a young philanthropic entrepreneur's enthusiasm!)

Besides basketball, I had one other driving passion during my youth. Had my parents discouraged it, my entire life would have been different. Instead, they allowed me to embrace it—a gift for which I shall forever remain grateful.

Before I entered my teen years, I had begun to seek refuge in a group of friends who opened my eyes to exciting new worlds. These kids lived lives of adventure, pushed themselves to excel beyond their natural limits, and weren't afraid to stand up for truth and justice. They didn't attend my school. And they didn't care that I was an outsider. They weren't even real people. They were the cast of characters inside my comic books. Soon, the loneliness of my youth and hunger for escapism culminated in a fascination with comics that ignited my entrepreneurial journey.

But it didn't start out like that. Far from it. There was no declaration of my life's mission, no clarion call from on high to pursue a corporate life. Business dreams seldom begin that way. Instead, like most entrepreneurial jumping-off points, my interest in comics was something I stumbled into based on my interests. As I always tell aspiring businesspeople that your passions are your spirit's compass. Don't ignore them. Take them seriously. Embrace them. I know I did. And in the end, that made all the difference.

Here's how it happened. Like many kids, I had always enjoyed Marvel and DC Comics' characters such as Batman, Spider-Man, and Superman. Battles between good and evil, action-packed heroics, untapped supernatural abilities—I loved how comics transported me to another realm. They were a welcome escape from reality.

Then in the early nineties a comic book company I had never heard of, named Valiant, blipped my radar. The people behind Valiant were legendary comic writer and former Marvel editor-in-chief Jim Shooter and renowned music manager Steve Massarsky. While Marvel and DC Comics were known at that time for their dazzling artwork, Valiant stood out for its edgy storytelling, deep character development, and often taboo, envelope-pushing themes and moral dilemmas. Immediately, I was hooked.

Three Valiant comic series gripped me the tightest. The first of these was Shadowman. Set in New Orleans, Louisiana, this voodoo-themed comic told the story of an aspiring jazz musician named Jack Boniface. After a boozy night with a woman he picked up from a jazz bar, Jack awoke from his blacked-out slumber and realized he'd been bitten on the neck. While trying to track down the woman who bit him, Boniface stumbled upon a discarded mask and slipped it on. Soon, the protagonist discovered newfound superpowers of lightning speed and agility, night vision, inhuman strength, limitless endurance, and above all-fearlessness.

Then Jack's voodoo-practising maid Nettie made him a black uniform to go with his skull-like mask. 'In voodoo talk, "shadow" means soul. You the Shadowman,' she declared. From then on, Shadowman fearlessly hunted down the worst of the worst—rapists, serial killers ... you name it, he stopped them. Something in the character's desire to confront fear and darkness head-on resonated with me. Even as a boy, that level of self-belief and courage was a virtue I desperately desired, but knew I'd yet to develop. Living vicariously through Shadowman acclimated me to the idea of running *towards* the things I feared, not slinking away in retreat.

Another favourite Valiant series of mine was *Eternal Warrior*. This comic was set before recorded history and recounted the tale of Gilad Anni-Padda, an immortal hero who traversed time using his superior understanding of martial strategy and tactics to defeat evil foes. The brother of Ivar the Timewalker and Armstrong (of the *Archer and Armstron*g comic series), Gilad also possessed regenerative powers to heal any battle wound. Because he was an eternal character, the comic portrayed Gilad as a relatively young hero who often led older men. The reason Gilad was chosen as leader of his tribe was because he was an unusually talented strategist. Known as the 'Fist and Steel', Gilad believed it was his calling to make the world a better place.

It wasn't until I began working on this book that I realized how deeply I had internalized lessons from this character. The idea that a younger man could emerge as a leader of older men by mastering the art of strategy burrowed itself into my subconscious. While I knew I would never have Gilad's stylish hair or cool aura, the character added a new word to my teenage lexicon—'strategy'—and informed me that honing it was a key that picked the lock of leadership, regardless of one's age.

But as much as *Shadowman* and *Eternal Warrior* meant to me as a kid, my all-time favourite comic series was Valiant's *Harbinger*. The series' hero and mine was a misfit teen named Peter Stanchek, also known as 'Sting'. Sting was one of the most powerful 'Harbingers' or 'psiots', a rare breed of humans with extraordinary psychic and mental powers on the planet. Wipe minds, control minds, project thoughts, telekinesis, teleportation—if it had to do with powers of the mind, Sting could do it.

Sting's arch nemesis was Toyo Harada, a Japanese corporate titan and the world's most powerful psiot. To the public, Harada appeared to be a benevolent philanthropist and caring businessman. In reality, Harada was an evil megalomaniac who had assembled the Harbinger Foundation, a syndicate of fellow psiots who could help him conquer the world in the name of saving the planet from itself. He sometimes called his team the 'Eggbreakers'—a reflection of his morally ambiguous belief that 'to make an omelette you have to break a few eggs'. Originally, Toyo Harada tried to recruit Sting to join his Harbinger Foundation. But when the teenager learned Harada had his best friend murdered, Sting assembled a group of psiots known as the Renegades to battle Harada and his minions.

I was drawn to the Peter Stanchek character for a myriad of reasons. For one, he was from Pittsburgh, the place where I, too, had lived for a time and felt misunderstood. Second, because he didn't understand his own natural gifts, Peter was treated like an outcast, gave into self-destructive behaviours, and yearned for a close-knit family, spiritual tranquillity and self-control. But the biggest thing that drew me to Sting was that the greater the stress he and his companions endured, the more they transcended their limits and unlocked latent mental powers.

One of my core beliefs—one of the drivers of my philosophy of the turnaround—is the deep conviction that every person contains vast reservoirs of untapped potential. If you don't believe humans have hidden abilities, you can never activate a turnaround. Why? Because you've accepted that their current state of 'failure' is the result of a flawed nature that is fixed, permanent, immutable.

If, however, you adopt the belief that pressure makes diamonds, you can lead others to realize that the 'fires' of life and business burn away the dross, purify us, and produce strengths we never realized were locked inside the vaults of our minds.

One of my most sacred beliefs is that thoughts become things, the latent becomes manifest. Would-be entrepreneurs shouldn't just guard their words, but their minds as well. The subconscious is extremely powerful. What you put in, you get out. I'm not suggesting you sell all your possessions and meditate on a mountainside. (Although sometimes after a bruising day in the boardroom that idea has tremendous appeal to me). We're all human; no one is perfect. But if I've learned anything along my entrepreneurial journey, it's that those who succeed are those who are mindful of their thoughts and the energy they surround themselves with. That's not psycho-babble or comic book psychiatry. It's just the truth. Ask any successful person and she or he will probably tell you the same thing.

As for my superhero Pete Stanchek, he went on to do many great things. But the grandest irony was this—as a teenager, I never knew what the word 'harbinger' in the title of my favourite comic series meant.

> ***harbinger*** *(noun) def: Something that foreshadows a future event; something that gives an anticipatory sign of what is to come.*

Sitting on my childhood bed in Hong Kong, immersed in the pages of my favorite Valiant comic books, I had no idea of what was to come.

Comic books opened my eyes and mind to fresh ideas, edgy and provocative imagery, and archetypal notions of courage, leadership, and virtue. But as much as I learned from reading comics, I learned far more by collecting, buying, trading, and selling them. I'll go even further: doing comic-book deals as a kid with classmates taught me more about entrepreneurship than just about anything else.

Back in the 1990s, when I first got really into comics, e-commerce and online shopping were nonexistent. So when I discovered a comic-book store in Hong Kong, I felt like I'd won the National Basketball Association (NBA) finals. Initially I would buy them and enjoy them alone. Then one day I told a classmate about a series I was reading. 'Sounds cool', he said. 'Maybe I'll check it out.' The next day I tucked a copy in my book bag and presented it to him. 'I had an extra copy, so this one's on me,' I told him. 'I hope you like it. Let me know.'

I'd almost forgotten about the whole thing until a few days later when he tapped me on the shoulder. 'How much do I owe you for the comic book?', he asked.

'Nothing,' I said. 'It's yours to keep. No charge.' He smiled. 'Well, do you have any more I can buy off you?'

That's how fast it happened.

No fancy business plan.

No sophisticated financial modelling.

No deep understanding of sales or marketing.

Nothing.

Just a kid who gave a classmate a comic book from his personal stash, sparked demand, and then became a supplier to meet the demand he'd triggered. That was the first of many steps on the path to creating a $100 million business and the third-largest superhero entertainment company in the world behind Marvel and DC Comics.

After that first sale, I went home and sorted my comic books into two piles: those I knew would increase in value, and those I was fine parting with. I would then hand the second pile out to guys at school.

But instead of slinging loose copies at random kids, I slipped them inside a nice cellophane bag with a cardboard backing and presented them in a way that suggested higher perceived value. They'd then read the free copy, get hooked, and come back and buy another from me. A micro market was born.

The comic-book trend spread like wildfire throughout our school. Soon kids started frequenting the same Hong Kong comic book store I'd found. Others with relatives in the US began having family members ship them popular books. When my dad travelled on short business trips to America I would have him bring me hard-to-find comics as well. Before long, a whole secondary comic-book market had mushroomed inside our school. That shifted the economic dynamics away from buying and selling and more towards doing trades.

The changing currents in our micro market—one I'd largely created out of thin air—meant I would have to learn new tricks to have the best collection on campus. And even though as a kid I had no idea what terms like 'relative value', 'arbitrage', or 'opportunity cost' meant, I was soon learning those and other business principles without even realizing it.

For me everything flowed from doing my research—something that remains true for me even today. First, I would study the comic book price guides. Then I would monitor prices over time to spot trends. What's hot? What's cold? Which issues and series were rising? Falling? I was an informational scavenger who gobbled up as much intel as I could. Next, I would do on-the-ground research to gauge which kids wanted certain comics the most. The stronger the intensity of their interest or desire, the greater the odds I could strike a favourable deal. Third, I would hunt for price gaps between what a book was worth, what I'd paid for it, and how I could trade comics with declining value for those with greater upside. None of this was difficult; all of it was easy, basic math. I was learning business by doing business.

Soon I discovered that many classmates, particularly those from wealthier families, didn't care all that much about studying pricing guides, researching demand, or worrying about profits or losses. For them comic books were a casual hobby, nothing more. If they got the books they wanted and enjoyed reading, they were happy. End of story.

But not for me. I was too passionate about comics to treat them as a casual interest. And that passion meant I actually enjoyed the process of researching prices and studying trends. None of it felt like 'work'. Far from it. Something about the thrill of the deal and the act of creating value—receiving something worth more than I paid for it—gave me an adrenaline rush.

I also found joy in the social dimensions of deal-making, as well as discussing and debating the coolest superheroes and story lines with classmates. One of those individuals was a fellow Indian expat who entered the seventh grade with me, named Dinesh Shamdasani—a bright kid who wore wire-rimmed coke-bottle glasses. Dinesh and I hit it off not too long after we met. Best of all, we shared a mutual passion for Valiant comics. It felt good to have a friend who understood Indian culture and liked the same things I did. Neither of us had any idea of what our love for Valiant would blossom into years later. Back then we were just two Indian kids having fun and trying to navigate through adolescent life in Hong Kong.

Because Dinesh studied comics like I did, we often shared in each other's excitement over new issues or a great trade one of us had made. One of those high points happened on a visit to see my Uncle Anil, a gold medallist heart surgeon, in Atlantic City, New Jersey. During my stay I made an impassioned pitch for him to take me to a popular comic-book store near the beach. The shop—and one particular comic book inside it—had caught my eye while walking.

'Uncle, you have to understand: this store has one of the hottest Valiant comic books in the world. I've been waiting an entire year for a chance like this.'

'How much does it cost?' he asked.

'Seventy dollars.'

'Seventy dollars?! For a kid's comic book? Are you serious?'

'You don't understand, Uncle. I can't buy this particular one in Hong Kong. I saved my money and waited all year. I've been dreaming about this.'

He raised an eyebrow and tepidly agreed.

'But tell me one thing, what in the world does one do with a seventy-dollar comic book?'

I grinned.

'You trade it for several more comic books worth ten times as much,' I said.

And that's exactly what I did. In fact, because that $70 comic book was so rare and impossible to find in Hong Kong, I ended up trading it for roughly $1,000 worth of other comic books. A valuable early lesson in return on investment or ROI.

If I could whisper one bit of entrepreneurial advice to parents, it would be: encourage your children to embrace their passions—and empower them to discover the business lessons embedded within. When you stop and think about it, just about *every* hobby—indeed, every physical *thing*—holds opportunities and insights for those who view the world through entrepreneurial eyes. And I'm not just talking about obvious things, like cars, technology, or real estate. Indeed, some of the biggest business wins are achieved by seizing small, relatively mundane markets.

Don't believe me?

Here, try this. Right now, let your eyes float up off this page and scan the room or area around you.

Go ahead.

Do it.

Those small rubber buttons over there on your TV remote control, the tiny screws that hold the hinge of the eyeglasses you or a family member wears, the printed labels emblazoned across the packaged foods inside your refrigerator—all of those everyday, 'boring' products made someone wealthy. Better yet, because those individuals took a risk and launched businesses, hundreds if not thousands of other people now have jobs. Opportunities are everywhere. The sooner you retrain your eyes to view the world through the prism of entrepreneurship, the sooner you can build up the courage to take those first small steps to start your own journey.

Like the Shadowman character I loved so much, I, too, had been 'bitten', but by the business bug. With my comic-book trading humming along, I wanted to learn more about business firsthand. So, at the age of fifteen, I asked my parents if I could get my first job. The idea was to learn a few basics, earn a little spending money, and gain some experience that would hopefully help land another good internship later on. My parents liked the idea and said I was free to begin my job hunt.

I had no idea where I would work or who would employ a teenager with zero skills. So I tried to think of things that aligned with my interests. Because I loved comics I also had a natural affinity for movies and entertainment. In Hong Kong, the film industry largely revolved around kung fu films. I'd always been a fan of Bruce Lee, but I knew next to nothing about the movie business. Still, I'd heard a major production and distribution company, called Media Asia Films, was located not too far from where we lived.

Through a family connection, I went to their office, filled out an application and got interviewed. When I learned I'd been hired, I was excited. When I learned who I would be working with, I could hardly believe it. Neither could my parents.

'Jackie Chan?' my mom asked.

'That's correct,' I said.

'As in Jackie Chan, the Karate guy?' my mom asked.

'Yep, Mom. But it's not Karate, it's kung fu.'

'The Jackie Chan that's in actual *movies*?'

'That's the one.'

'And you're sure that this is real?'

'Mom ... yes! It's real. They told me I will be assisting Mr Chan while he's on set shooting films.'

The fact that I would be little more than a glorified towel boy didn't matter. I would get to observe and learn about the entertainment world up close and personal. Better yet, I would also be working for one of the coolest martial artists in the world. I couldn't wait to start.

When I first met Jackie I hardly recognized him. He was in plain clothes and had yet to get into wardrobe and makeup. He looked tough as nails and no-nonsense—a drastic departure from his onscreen fun-loving, family-guy persona. The rest of the day, my heart pounded like a hammer inside my chest. I remember thinking: *whatever you do, don't mess up or do anything stupid.*

Lucky for me, the job initially consisted of running simple errands and fetching anything Jackie wanted or needed. Once filming started, Jackie morphed into character. He was the consummate professional. He was deeply committed to entertaining people with the slapstick action and family-value themes audiences have grown to love. That meant he took his craft seriously. He knew his lines by heart. Not surprisingly, he nailed his stunts and fight scenes as well. One thing surprised me, though. The director made Jackie repeat kicks and punches over and over so that the cameras could pick them up at different angles. Instead of a fluid, seamless choreographed fight sequence, things on set felt interrupted, with lots of starts and stops. Still, getting to see it all behind the scenes was a real treat.

I remember, one day, famed Hollywood director and producer Brett Ratner came on set to show us a movie trailer. It was for the blockbuster *Rush Hour* film series that he had directed, featuring Jackie and comedy star Chris Tucker. Brett asked us, 'Well, what do you guys think?'

I thought it looked terrible, so I stayed quiet. I'm glad I did, because the *Rush Hour* movie series turned out to be one of the most successful action-comedy sequel series. (Shows how much I knew!) But as fate would have it, fifteen years later, I would cross paths with Brett Ratner again, as a partner on a film project.

After several weeks on the job, my duties expanded to reviewing Media Asia Films' contracts. And that's when I got my first glimpse at just how big of a business nerd I was destined to become. As a fifteen-year-old kid, I found poring over media distribution contracts utterly and completely mesmerizing. (A dorkier sentence has probably never been written in the annals of human history, but it's the absolute truth). The percentages, the terms, the legalese, I was hypnotized by all of it; I wanted to understand everything. Luckily, I had a kind supervisor who patiently entertained my litany of questions.

My first job reinforced at least two truths. First, celebrities are regular people just like everyone else. And second, the business side of media and entertainment is a labyrinth of contracts and concepts. I found it fascinating and wanted to learn more about it in college.

After working with Media Asia, I wanted to continue exploring the world of work. I'd scanned the job classified page of the newspaper almost every day and dreamed of how I might one day land a top position. But then there, in fine print, almost every job listing clearly stated that a college degree and prior experience were required. *How can I have prior experience if all the jobs require prior experience!*

Try as I might, after reading through hundreds of ads, I couldn't find a job for a student that did not require a college degree. And then I saw it: the American Chamber of Commerce (ACC) publishing department had a single opening for an editorial assistant for a two-month summer position. My persistence in hunting for a viable job opportunity paid off; I got the job. The editor-in-chief explained that my work for Media Asia and writing skills stood out on my job application. He also liked that Media Asia had given me a good recommendation letter—I learned how one experience can build off another.

As for the job itself, I didn't mind that I wasn't provided a desk and had to instead sit on a stool in the pantry. As a teen, they were offering me an exciting opportunity to learn new things and gain valuable experience—assets that would be critical for landing future jobs and getting into a great college. To do that, though, I needed to put my high school education front and centre, get better grades, and make responsible choices.

But that plan came to a screeching halt when later that year I left for the Hell-Ville boarding school in the US. After all the altercations and physical fights there—and being exposed to the school's seedy underground culture—I returned to Hong Kong a hardier, more worldly sixteen-year-old.

Over the four years to come, the sweet and gentle kid I had once been morphed into a selectively aggressive young man, with a knack for making poor life choices. The worst of these were yet to come.

2

Mistakes Can Be a Gift

LYING IN A hospital bed, I awoke to the faint sound of muffled voices. My eyes fluttered open and I saw tubes snaked over my arms and across my chest. How I had gotten there or why, I wasn't sure.

What happened? I thought. *What's going on?*

I rotated my pounding head to the left. A terminally ill-looking man lay motionless. I turned my head to the right. Another man, equally badly off, lay still.

My eyes scanned the dimly lit room before stopping on a wall clock. It was about a half-hour before midnight.

Blurry scenes from hours before began flashing through my foggy mind.

A group of my Hong Kong friends ... the basketball court in the public park ... a bottle of gin ... a taxi.

A nurse walked in the room. I asked if I could make a phone call and dialled up one of my friends.

'What the hell happened?' I asked.

'What do you mean?' he said.

'I'm in the hospital.'

'The hospital?'

'Yeah, I'm in the ICU.'

'I have no idea. The last we saw you was at the basketball court when you got in the taxi.'

'Why did I take a taxi?'

'Don't you remember? You said you had some kind of a SAT class or something. So we helped you into the taxi.'

'Well then, why am I in the hospital?!'

'I don't know, man! I'm telling you. The taxi was the last we saw you in.'

Almost as soon as I got off the phone a doctor stopped by my bed to check on me.

'Doctor, can you please tell me what happened?', I asked.

'What do you mean what happened?' he replied.

'How did I get to the hospital?'

'A taxi driver dropped you off here. You passed out in his cab.'

I looked down at my hospital gown.

'Well, may I leave now and go home?'

'Are you kidding? Of course you can't leave. You had your stomach pumped. You had alcohol poisoning. I don't know how much you drank, but from the looks of things it was a lot. Jason, this is serious.'

My heart started hammering. I needed to call my parents. Fast.

My mother answered the phone. I started in with a lame excuse. She cut me off.

'Stop. Just stop! Your friend already called and told us the truth. The police station has your bag. We'll pick it up later. We're coming up to the hospital now.'

I sat in silence waiting for my parents to arrive. It felt like someone had bored a hole in my stomach with a drill. Whether that was from the pumping or anxiety over my parents' arrival, I can't say. I watched the wall clock tick.

The mental gaps from the day's events slowly started filling in. I'd been at the basketball court with the guys I started hanging out with after I had returned to Hong Kong from Hell-Ville. They were rebels. I now felt most at home as part of their group. Still, there was a limit to how far I was willing to go. So when they said they planned to steal from a nearby convenience store, I hung back.

When they returned, they handed me a one litre bottle of gin from the large collection of stolen items. I'd never drank hard liquor before, only beer. 'We got that one for you. Go ahead. Drink it,' one of them said. 'Just drink from the bottle,' said another. After the first scorching swallow, I tried to pass the bottle off. 'Nah, man. That's yours. Drink the whole thing.'

There we sat, swigging stolen booze by the basketball court, me taking gulp after gulp of straight gin until I drank the whole thing. I tottered, howled like an idiot, stumbled, fell, and smashed the empty bottle on the pavement. Apparently, according to my friend on the phone, I'd then told the guys I had to get to a SAT class. (I didn't remember that part). The fact that I thought I could sit through a SAT class shows just how inebriated I must have been. Thank God for that cab driver who took mercy on me and drove me to the hospital.

When my parents arrived, they reacted more with disappointment than anger. It cut much deeper. But sadly, it wasn't enough to shake me from my stupidity. In truth, while they were there with me in the hospital, all I could think about was whether they had retrieved my book bag from the police and discovered what was inside. Soon after hanging out with this group, I became a smoker. When the guys tossed me a stolen pack of smokes, I'd tucked them in my bag.

I wish I could tell you that downing a stolen bottle of gin, getting alcohol poisoning, landing in the hospital, and having my stomach pumped was enough to jerk me back on track. But it wasn't. I was in a bad place heading nowhere fast. At sixteen, my tumble into the abyss had only just begun.

Among other things, Hong Kong is known for its vast network of gangs. Indeed, gangs and drugs weren't hard to find almost anywhere in Hong Kong in the nineteen-eighties and nineties. Teenagers were regularly recruited to do dirty work and sell and transport drugs, sometimes in conjunction with corrupt police. Thankfully I steered clear of all that and never joined a gang. But the same couldn't be said for several of the guys I hung out with. Gang membership brought respect. It also meant that if anyone messed with them, there was a crew to have their back in a fight. And of course, there was the money that came with drug trafficking—something I quickly realized was far more prevalent than I'd ever understood. It wasn't uncommon to be talking with a guy and glance down and see heroin in his sock. Sadly, two friends later had drug-related deaths.

It was only a matter of time before I got in a scuffle with the wrong person. I was done with taking things on the chin. After being my bully's punching bag at Hell-Ville, I'd adopted a different plan. If someone hit me, I was going to hit them back. Harder.

Sure enough, one day at school I got into an argument with a guy. When he swung at my face, I cocked my fist back and cracked him right in the eye, before tagging him with two jabs to the chin. The vice principal spotted us from a distance. 'Stop!' he yelled as he hustled to break through the crowd encircling us. But it was too late. I'd already publicly humiliated my rival. The boy got a black eye. I got detention. But it was what he said walking away that chilled me to the bone.

He looked me dead in the eyes and said, 'You're going to pay for this.'

I later learned he belonged to a gang. This, in turn, made me more eager to befriend and hang out with guys who could provide backup when needed. That 'protection' could also extend to my friends.

I remember when we were sixteen, Dinesh started getting picked on. The instigator threatened to have a group of guys jump him. I intervened and stopped him from starting a fight with my friend, but I knew things weren't over. I told some gang-affiliated guys we had a problem. They found Dinesh's bully, hauled him to the school bathroom, and pounded him. That wasn't my intention; I just wanted them to back him off. But we now had a new problem. The boy they'd beaten was himself part of a crew. There was no way that crew would let the fight go unanswered.

I was on guard. Reprisals could come at any time—often when you least expected. A friend had invited me to a party but I couldn't make it. I later found out the same kid who got beaten up in the bathroom had also been invited and had fifteen guys waiting to ambush me and smash bottles on my head and land me in the hospital. Another bullet dodged.

Somehow, despite all my teenage chaos, I managed to graduate high school with pretty good grades and got accepted to a few American universities. In 1999, I headed off to Boston, Massachusetts, to attend a small college which had given me a partial scholarship. I was ready to get out of Hong Kong. I thought maybe a change of scenery would get me on the right track. Instead, the bad traits I'd formed in high school just came with me to college. My environment wasn't the problem. I was. My inner game ruled my outer game.

At college I formed friends quickly and found the campus welcoming to international students. I even began dating my first girlfriend. But inside, I was toxic. I went to nightclubs and got in fights. At college bars, I ordered *quadruple* whiskies and Coke. My alcohol tolerance was alarming. Still, I didn't realize how extreme it had gotten. On New Year's, I blacked out and had to be carried home by three buddies. Did that jolt me into self-awareness? Nope. I just rationalized my behaviour as normal college mischief. *Big deal,* I told myself. *Everyone lets loose in college.* I was lost in a haze of self-delusion.

Why am I telling you all this and airing my dirty laundry?

Because one of the biggest myths is the false belief I see that business is only for the well-heeled and flawless, people with no human failings or personal struggles. That's bullshit. Authentic entrepreneurs will tell you they've failed more times than they've succeeded. And I'm not just talking about risk-taking ventures and corporate start-ups.

Entrepreneurs often come from broken homes, have battled insecurities, dropped out of school, struggled with addiction, had their hearts crushed by the loves of their lives, had people tell them they'd amount to nothing. And yet. They got their interior house in order, swatted away the haters, and let their mistakes fuel their successes. Everyone stumbles. It's how you pick yourself and grow from it that matters.

Here's what I need you to understand: *money will only make you more of what you already are.*

Go back and reread that sentence and marinate your mind on its meaning.

Financial success amplifies whatever is already inside your spirit. If you're at peace with yourself and filled with joy and concern for others, you'll use your wealth and influence to improve the lives of others and make the world a better place. If, however, you're still battling inner demons, money will only inflame them and make them bigger. Had I made my first million dollars when I was in college, I would have crashed and burned. No question about it. My inner game wasn't ready for wealth. But here's the coolest part, something I began to discover later in college: entrepreneurship is one of the best 'gyms' in which to work out your personal issues.

Two comments, both of them from family members, sparked the epiphany that helped me start to turn it all around.

It happened on a trip home from college over a holiday. Even though my parents didn't know the extent of my smoking, fighting, and drinking, they had seen enough to know I was haplessly careening through college. When they called me, I was despondent. When they asked me about my goals and career plans, I lacked vision or ambition. After a few days of being back in Hong Kong, Mom, Dad, Neil, and his then-girlfriend (now wife) Arthi were having dinner at home. That's when the conversation started.

'So Jason, we haven't seen you do much studying while you've been home,' my father said.

'I've done some,' I said.

'I haven't seen it,' said my mother.

'I'm on break. I don't need to be studying all the time,' I said defensively.

'Well you certainly find time to be on the phone a lot,' said my father.

'I have a girlfriend, Dad. We miss each other and want to keep in touch over the break,' I said.

'Does she go to all those parties you go to?' my mom asked.

I sighed.

'May I please be excused? I need to use the restroom.'

As I was washing my hands in the restroom, I could hear my parents talking in hushed tones. I stepped softly down the hallway to listen to what they were saying. And that's when I heard my mother say the words that lit a thousand fires under me.

'I'm concerned. Very concerned. He's never going to reach his potential,' my mother told the family. 'He doesn't have it in him. We thought college would make him better. Instead, it's made him worse.'

I rounded the corner into the dining room in a huff.

'Do you think I can't hear you? Why do you have to find fault in everything I do? I'm finally having fun and am happy. Can't you just accept that and be glad for me?'

My mother's words seared me to the core. I was angry. That night it was all I could think about. But once I calmed down, I had to confront the truth—my parents were right and I was wrong. I owed more not just to myself, but to my family. My parents weren't independently wealthy. They worked hard and saved all their lives just so Neil and I could attend quality schools. The more I reflected on my mother's words, the more I opened my eyes to a glaring reality.

Many of the kids I'd met at school in Boston came from wealthy families who owned serious companies and had major league connections. For them, college was a playground, a place to have fun while checking an obligatory box on their resumés before returning to guaranteed careers working for their family businesses. Whether they graduated at the top or bottom of the class, it didn't matter. They had a fat inheritance waiting for them or the safety net of a trust fund underneath them. But the same wasn't true for me—and my parents were wise enough to know it. There was no family empire to fall back on, no platinum parachute to catch me and bring me in for a soft landing if I fell. As an exceptional educator, my mother knew school was the key that could unlock doors for me. But only if I was willing to do the work and walk through them.

The next morning over breakfast, Arthi and I talked about the conversation from the night before.

'Mom and Dad just love you, that's all,' she said gently. 'They just want what's best for you.'

'I know,' I said.

And then she said the words that zoomed my vision into focus.

'Jason, you just need to ask yourself: where are you now, what do you want to do, and how are you going to get there from today.'

For whatever reason, my sister-in-law's simple, well-intentioned, future-focused statement, sparked a level of clarity and direction I'd lacked. Where am I now, what do I want to do, and how am I going to get there starting from today? Whatever my answers, they would serve as a roadmap to give me clear goals and a path to achieve them. For the next few weeks, I meditated my mind on this and another challenging self-reflection:

If, Jason, you say you value family, you have a responsibility to all your ancestors, for the cumulative sacrifices they have made for you to have the life you have today, as well as your future wife and children, you should begin honouring them through your actions right now, not just later. They all deserve better than what you've given.

Sting, Shadowman, and Eternal Warrior couldn't have said it any better.

The next year in 2000, I moved to Carnegie Mellon University (CMU) in Pittsburgh, Pennsylvania—the place I'd lived briefly as a child. The decision wasn't easy. I left some of the best friends I'd made in my life to that point. But I knew for my new mindset to take root, I needed a fresh start.

When I arrived at CMU, I embarked on a radical personal makeover. If I'd been extreme in my vices, I reasoned I could become equally extreme in my virtues. It began with getting my physical body in shape. Fitness became my new passion. Before then, I hadn't really spent significant time in a gym. I didn't have money for a trainer, so I started simple. My goal was to learn a new exercise each day and strive to do more repetitions than I did the day before.

I began doing 10 push-ups a day. Each day I would boost it another 10 push-ups and spread them out throughout my day. I refused to miss a single day; I forced myself to keep going, no matter what. Within a few months, I began adding more and more push-ups to my daily target before finally working up to 1,000 push-ups a day. (Coincidentally, I later realized that one of my favourite comic book villains—Bane from the Batman series—had done the same!)

I applied the same level of discipline to academics. My daily scholastic mantra was to attend every class, complete all homework in advance to stay ahead, take detailed notes during lectures, ask professors questions if you don't understand, and leave nothing to chance. Then I added my own extreme twist on things, I denied myself food until I was finished completing homework assignments. The same for sleep, no rest until you finish studying for the test.

I received a B- on my first English paper. My professor said she knew I could do better. I asked her how. She helped sharpen my writing skills. The next paper I received a B, then a B+, and finally A+. Suddenly I was acing every paper. My goal was perfection. Nothing less.

I imposed other extreme goals on myself. I wanted to test my mental limits (I was in full Harbingers mode!). For example, I started timing myself on math problems to force myself to do things faster and better. If an exam lasted two hours, I wanted to complete it in one hour so I could take the exam twice to double-check every answer to ensure it was a 100 per cent accurate. Once I got in the rhythm and made excellence a habit, I discovered that I didn't have to work as hard to ace things.

And of course the vices that had long bedevilled me—drinking, smoking, fighting—I stopped completely. I had seen and done it all before, so I now had the self-assurance to stand up to peer pressure and make better choices. Quitting smoking cold turkey was difficult, but I did it. And I focused on not just purifying my physical body, but my thoughts and spirit as well. I avoided gossip and negative energy. I exerted the same control over my own thoughts—focusing on positive and uplifting ideas.

My approach might best be summed up by the quote on the Tupac Shakur poster that hung in my dingy Pittsburgh apartment. It read: 'I believe that everything you do comes back to you. So everything that I do that's bad, I'm going to suffer from it. But in my mind, I believe what I'm doing is right. So I feel like I'm going to heaven.'

I loved it. It was a simple reminder that bad choices and thoughts are like a boomerang—they always come back and hit you. So I did my best to elevate myself a little each day.

Another thing that spurred my motivation for self-improvement during college and beyond was discovering and tapping into my spirituality. Growing up, my family wasn't religious. So I began reading books on the world's great religions, including learning about India's unparalleled spiritual history. I wanted to learn about others' belief systems—their principles and values—and to understand what is a 'great man'. Then one day I was talking to my Uncle Anil about all the work I was doing on myself, how I was striving to live a better, cleaner life, and the beliefs I had formed through experience and reflection. Impressed, he said, 'It sounds like you've concluded many of Jainism's core ideas on your own.' He explained to me that our family's ancestral origins were deeply rooted in it.

I started reading books on Buddhist and Jain beliefs. I was particularly captivated by Jainism's central tenet that the purpose of souls is to reach their spiritual potential, which is infinite and God-like, and to minimize harm to all living beings and help one another. My days of adding toxicity and disharmony to the world were over. I wanted to live a more hopeful existence, one where my purpose was to eventually help others. The idea that one could achieve inner peace through a continuous process of refining and improving oneself held great appeal to me.

Then based on a friend's recommendation, I studied the story and spiritual teachings of Sai Baba from Shirdi. His life, the miracles he performed, the wisdom in his writings—I treasured it all. I wasn't sure exactly where Shirdi was located in India, or who might serve as a tour guide to help me find it, but I resolved that one day I would find out and make the visit. Leaning on faith would later prove vital in times of personal tragedy. But for the time being, my focus was putting my newfound purpose-driven life to good use in college.

I was slowly becoming a better version of myself. Still, I made the decision early on not to tell my parents about the 'new and improved' version of their son. I wanted to show them results. Needless to say, the straight A+'s, and being one of the best students at the university, made them quite pleased. After years of wandering in the wilderness, I was finally focused and working towards a future.

Soon, I had professors and others telling me I should consider transferring to top schools like Harvard and Wharton at the University of Pennsylvania. I applied to both and got waitlisted at Harvard and accepted to Wharton. I decided to pursue a business degree at Wharton. There, I would learn lessons and forge friendships that would make my entrepreneurial dreams finally take flight.

Wharton was in a league all its own, a gathering of some of the world's finest business minds. I was humbled and grateful for the opportunity to attend a storied institution that had produced leaders across all sectors of business. It was also a little intimidating. I continued my 'all business' study regimen, and added in a few more of my extreme personal experiments. I even tried listening to audio books while I slept to see if I could soak up extra knowledge.

One thing I found a little surprising was that my fascination with entrepreneurship—learning how to create something from nothing by learning all facets of business—was not the dominant goal for many of my colleagues. At that time, most seemed more interested in investment banking, management consulting, private equity, or hedge fund investing. But for me, there was something exhilarating about approaching business from a holistic, 360-degree perspective to learn every aspect of what creates a winning company.

Entrepreneurs can't do it any other way. When you're just starting out and struggling and bootstrapping, you don't have the capital to hire a team of specialists. That means you have to figure out each and every piece of business—strategy, product or service development, management, finance, operations, marketing, investor relations—all by yourself.

To borrow an Olympics analogy, entrepreneurship is a little like the decathlon; instead of specializing in a single sport like football or boxing, competitors must master multiple disciplines, the confluence of which makes up their total overall performance. Understanding how all the dimensions of business interlock with one another and then applying that knowledge seemed like a giant obstacle course. I wanted to learn how to conquer it and gain some first-hand business exposure across these different areas. I'm a big believer in students pursuing internship opportunities. The 'dip your toe in to test the waters' mindset can be extremely useful when it comes to discovering your passions in life—as well as dispelling career myths one may hold erroneously. As I often tell parents, broad exposure is important, particularly for younger aspiring entrepreneurs. As for me, every chance I got during my college years I did an internship with a different company.

One of my earliest internships was with Merrill Lynch. Finance had always struck me as a glamorous, high-paying job that would make for a dream career. Boy, was I wrong! Within two weeks of working as part of their research team I was ready to quit. The whole thing felt one-dimensional. I just stared at numbers all day; it was so theoretical. I wanted to get my hands dirty and do the actual work of business. But without my Merrill Lynch internship, I would have probably gone on believing my perception of finance as a jet-set career was accurate. I'm glad I did it!

My next internship was with McKinsey. That year I'd applied to dozens of companies including A.T. Kearney and Booz Allen, even though many had no formal internship program and therefore didn't hear back from most of them. I was excited, however, when I got an interview confirmation from McKinsey. It turned out that their Hong Kong office had many employees going on summer holiday and that they needed extra support.

My interview had been a mess. At nineteen, I didn't have great answers for their questions about logistics and financial services. Still, when they asked questions I didn't know how to answer, I stressed that I was a quick learner and hard worker and was willing to do whatever it took to contribute and add value. Up to that point McKinsey didn't hire college students or have internship programs globally, so when they told me I got the position, I became one of the youngest people in the company. Once again, good old-fashioned grit, determination, and persistence paid off. Landing the McKinsey position was a wonderful confidence booster for a nineteen-year-old.

The next holiday, I decided to work in public relations (PR) and advertising with Ogilvy & Mather. With the Merrill Lynch and McKinsey experiences under my belt, I thought I had a knockout resumé. To put it bluntly, I had an inflated ego and was arrogant. That's when the universe dealt me a whopping dose of humility.

I worked on the PR side (Ogilvy PR Worldwide) and later its advertising division (O&M). One of my assignments on the PR side was to try my hand at writing a speech for one of Ogilvy's clients, the CEO of one of the biggest theme parks in Hong Kong—Ocean Park. I was determined to craft the most eloquent oration ever. I spent hours drafting, editing, and polishing every sentence to make the speech sparkle.

On the day the CEO was to deliver the speech, I took a bus packed with journalists to the venue. When the big press conference started, the CEO was supposed to step up to the microphone and recite my expertly crafted speech script announcing all the park's new attractions and rides. But after a few sentences, I realized something wasn't right. The CEO had scrapped my speech entirely. Not a single word he spoke was mine. I wasn't just disappointed. I was humbled. And better off for it!

One of my later internships took place in the US for The Conference Board—a think tank that disseminates its research to large companies and CEOs. I was grateful when I was selected for one of only two positions for their economics department where, years earlier, Alan Greenspan had worked. My boss was tasked with releasing the Consumer Confidence Index (CCI), data that has a large impact on businesses and stock markets. My job was to serve as an internal consultant to recommend how The Conference Board could optimize its research to more effectively serve clients.

After compiling my results, I faced a moral dilemma—if I was honest on how to improve, some people might lose their jobs. It was my first brush with the agonizing pain that comes from downsizing. I couldn't sleep. Ultimately I concluded that it was important to be intellectually honest about what construed the organization's long-term interests.

Several years later I came to know the head of the department. She told me they had incorporated many of my reorganization recommendations across the division. On the one hand, I was happy to know my work had proven helpful. On the other hand, I worried whether my work had cost people their jobs. It was a sobering experience, one that taught me to always take my job seriously. You never know how your work may have a bigger, long-term impact on a business and its people.

My two final internship opportunities were my first forays into governmental public affairs. One was for a lobbyist delegation in Washington DC, that represented American businesses. Given my age and lack of governmental experience, I knew I wouldn't have much to contribute. So I devoted myself to taking detailed notes during meetings, to establish a comprehensive report of the activities completed. That was my first interaction with politicians. I saw firsthand how the decisions they made had long-lasting and massive effects on the lives of the citizens they represented.

Seeing politicians up close also made me realize they are people just like anyone. That experience impressed upon me the fact that people generally fall into one of two categories—people who want to be spectators and are fine with others driving things, and those who want to be participants and play a role in shaping events. Neither is right or wrong, of course. It's about knowing yourself. But generally, I find that the second group tends to have the personality traits of entrepreneurs.

After my window into Washington, I was fortunate enough to be offered the opportunity to join the board of an established national non-profit. But it was a sobering experience. As a college student, I didn't have the kinds of capabilities, skills, insights, and experience to make an impact and offer maximum value. I realized if I couldn't uniquely contribute I may actually be taking the place of someone who could. No matter how passionate I might be about a social cause or policy, without the experience and resources to effectuate real change, I couldn't bring much to the table. I promised that later in life I would revisit social causes I was passionate about, after gaining the skills, relationships, and resources to enable me to contribute significantly.

Each of these internship experiences served as useful reminders that I still had much, much more to learn and experience. Every person thinks that they are doing very important work, sometimes not really understanding or appreciating the work of others. My business internships impressed upon me that one should understand that everyone is adding value and doing important work in the own way—and that should always be respected.

As for my personal life at Wharton, although I was busy making new friends, I still kept in touch with my childhood friend Dinesh. He attended University of Southern California's School of Cinema-Television to study filmmaking. We were both busy with school but made time to talk on the phone or through email. Even though we were older, we were both still comic book enthusiasts.

I'd gone from bad to good in the personal decisions I made as an angst-ridden teenager and used personal fitness as a healthy alternative outlet for stress and aggression. Through strict self-discipline and an extreme compulsion to improve, I'd turned around my grades and put receiving A+'s on autopilot—a crucial shift that got me into Wharton.

I wanted to continue stoking the fire inside to keep it burning bright.

But since when does anything go according to plan?

3

Limits Are Illusions

I COULDN'T SLEEP. My eyes lasered up into the ceiling. Lying on my bed inside my dumpy college apartment, thoughts, like fists, pounded my mind.

I needed to get away and rebuild myself. I had contracted an illness, setting off a month-long battle. The medical bills wiped out my bank funds, as the health insurance company used a loophole to not cover my hefty treatment cost. Equally devastating, though, was the mental and physical toll that sickness took on my body and spirit. While my doctors said I had fully recovered in near record time, I wanted to reignite that sense of confidence that had ebbed as my immune system had deteriorated.

Even before my first job as Jackie Chan's assistant, I'd been interested in martial arts. So, I browsed online and began researching training camps. Secretly, my plight may have given me an excuse to finally pursue an unfulfilled lifelong interest and push myself to another extreme challenge.

I found myself drawn to Muay Thai. I'd read that among the world's various marital arts styles—Brazilian jiu jitsu, kung fu, taekwondo, etc.—it was the most effective and rigorous fighting form. If I was going to do this, I wanted to do it right the first time around. That meant learning from the best from day one so as not to pick up any bad habits.

After reviewing several camps in Thailand, I came across what was reportedly one of the best places to train. Located a couple of hours outside Bangkok, the camp had been the training home for some of the world's greatest champion fighters. It was regarded as sort of the 'Harvard' of fight academies. The minute I read about it and saw the pictures, I knew that's where I wanted to go and immediately started planning a trip. With my Wharton classes finished for a while, I packed my bags and hopped onto a flight to Thailand to spend the summer there.

I rolled into the camp at night. After meandering through narrow rural roads, my cab driver pulled up and parked. Guarding the entrance was a big gate with barbed wire. The place looked like a prison.

What the hell did I sign myself up for? I remember thinking. *Is this even safe?*

I slung my bag full of gear over my shoulder and walked through the darkness to enter the camp. At intake, I was placed in a common room before being shown around. The training areas echoed with slaps from leather gloves and feet smacking punching bags and bodies. The facility was spartan by design. At the time, this was certainly no resort; more like an army barracks. Walking by a dining table I noticed that meals appeared sparse. We would eat what we were given and little else.

Before long I was introduced to a cast of characters who were as diverse as they were dangerous. There were roughly forty fighters in residence. They fell into several categories. First, you had the native professional Thai fighters who lived and trained in the camp year round, including a couple who were local fighting champions. Roughly half the men there belonged to this group. If they got married, their wives could reside with them. These men lived their lives like thoroughbred racehorses in a perpetual state of training and conditioning.

Next were foreigners like me who had come to train for different reasons. A few had law-enforcement backgrounds. One guy was from San Francisco, California—a detective and a SWAT team member. Another man was about to become a police officer in Chicago, Illinois. Then on the other end of the spectrum were people with more 'colourful' backgrounds. (I slept with a screwdriver and a knife under my pillow just in case.) One fighter hailed from Chicago and had previously been a major drug dealer. He had tattoos with the names of all his friends who had been killed. Outside of the US fighters, there were also several professional kickboxers from Amsterdam, England, and Spain.

Finally, there were our trainers. Our head trainer was a true legend of the sport, Apidej Sit Hirun. Considered the hardest kicker in Muay Thai history, Apidej was known as the 'golden leg'. He was so renowned, in fact, that the king of Thailand had crowned him the country's 'Fighter of the Century' and had a statue erected in his honour. During the prime of his fighting career, which spanned the sixties and the seventies, Apidej held seven championship titles simultaneously. He had gone an entire decade without losing a fight. Then, the day before he got married, he suffered defeat—forcing him to attend his own wedding beaten and bruised. In total, he had won 350 fights with only ten losses.

His humility matched his lethality. You would have never guessed he was the greatest fighter of all time. His warm, kind, quiet demeanour made you forget you were standing in front of one of the most dangerous martial artists on the planet. But he was. Indeed, throughout his fighting career, he had broken men's bones, forced others into early retirement, and killed no less than five men in the ring.

Another one of my trainers was known as the 'Wooden Man'. Also a champion fighter at his peak, he had earned his nickname because he could absorb maximum punishment without slowing his intensity or ferocity. Now, he was determined to instil that type of physical toughness in us, regardless of our skill level or experience.

The broad exposure to so many different fighters from diverse backgrounds, experiences, and geographies was eye-opening and educational on multiple levels. As these men pushed themselves and me to the physical breaking point (literally), I found myself learning lessons that applied to business that I never anticipated.

The first morning of training began with a 'warm up' run. This was a five-mile run performed at the speed of a sprint. The first time I did it, my stomach cramped so hard I thought I was going to pass out from all the heaving and panting while trying to catch my breath.

'Okay, men,' said Wooden Man, 'now that you've had a light warm-up we can get started with today's training.'

A 'light warm-up'! Is this guy freaking joking right now? What the trainer did not tell us was that this five-mile 'warm-up' sprint would be completed not once, but *twice* every single day.

Next up were kicking and punching exercises, often completed with the other fighters watching you. Given my novice (nonexistent) Muay Thai boxing skills, I knew virtually nothing about proper kicking technique. Now, I was going to do kicking drills in front of some of the world's greatest fighting champions. What could possibly go wrong?

'Kothari, you're up,' the trainer said.

I walked into the centre of the mat. The other fighters stood around the edges watching.

'Now go ahead and show us your kick,' said Wooden Man.

I steadied myself and took a deep breath. But as I sprung my right foot off the ground to snap off a kick, my left grounding foot wobbled, making my kicking leg squiggle through the air like a wet noodle.

The other fighters laughed.

It was embarrassing. But I wasn't there to impress anyone. I was there to learn.

Screw it, I said in my head. *Ignore the laughs. Just keep going. Figure out what you're doing wrong.*

'Okay,' I said to no one in particular. 'Someone tell me what am I doing wrong here?'

'It's your angle,' said one fighter standing beside the mat.

'Yeah,' said another, 'You need to kick on an angle like this.' He then demonstrated a kick using perfect technique.

'Try it again,' said Wooden Man.

I snapped another kick, this one slightly less awkward but still nowhere near correct.

'Nope, nope, nope,' said Wooden Man. 'Let me show you.'

The tough-as-nails trainer then stood in front of me, mirrored my stance, cocked his leg, and fired off a lightning fast foot strike.

'You see, you keep your hip down like this,' he explained.

I threw more kicks and heard more chuckles. I still didn't have it. Many of these guys, particularly the Thai fighters, had been training since they were five-years-old. Muay Thai was ingrained in their culture. To see a grown man not be able to perform a kick they had mastered as schoolboys must have been comical.

A couple of weeks later, though, something changed. Suddenly, it clicked; the angle worked. After a few more strikes using the proper technique, I got the power. I remember when it happened, because the giggles turned to cheers from a couple of the more seasoned fighters. It was a turning point.

Everything I managed to do in life up to that point was not based on some inherent talent or genius. I was just crazy determined. I went from bad to good in basketball, personal responsibility, and grades all by applying the same approach—hard work and thoughtful execution—to every area I wanted to improve. Now I was learning to do the same with kickboxing. Each day we performed hundreds of kicks. Soon, mine were quite powerful. All it took was ridiculous tenacity—and not caring if I looked silly while learning. Before long, I was really getting into it.

Then one day we were told it was time to begin sparring with a partner. They paired me up with a professional fighter. My heart raced.

At first, the whole thing felt unnatural. It's one thing to fight a man because you have some sort of beef with him. It's quite another when someone who did nothing wrong is looking at you and saying, 'Go ahead … punch and kick me.' The logical part of your brain says: *Why would I punch and kick him? He didn't do anything to deserve it.*

But civilized and conditioned politeness goes flying out the window the second a dude lands a thundering elbow to your chin or a crushing knee to your kidney.

Son of a @#$!%, that hurt! your mind yells. *Kick his ass … NOW!*

Nothing will motivate you to fight hard like taking a few strikes to the face. And that's exactly what happened. My primal instincts kicked in and I went after him.

After the first few rounds of sparring with a makeshift audience of fighters, I began to settle down, my shyness dissipated. Given his skill level, this was a David versus Goliath situation. To have any hope of surviving, I would need to apply strategic thinking to my fighting style. Thoughts and opportunities bubbled up in my head. Things like: *I'm a little taller than him, so let me stay at a distance ... Oh wait, I'm good at kicking with my right foot, so let me be at this angle.* Soon I was selecting punch and kick combinations like chess moves.

And I ended up being not half bad. I even landed some blows that hurt my opponent quite badly. In the end, a match that should have been one-sided ended up being a draw. The experience left a lasting impression on me about how strategy and lateral thinking can compensate for lesser capabilities. Still, despite my improvements, I remained in awe of how the top guys had perfected their craft. They were true experts at the highest level of their field, no different than my Wharton professors. They were just in different areas.

I believe life and learning are interconnected. Every human has potential. The key is figuring out how to unlock that potential and apply it in other areas. If you pay attention, you begin to see patterns emerge. By utilizing a common approach of focused intensity and rigour, you can surmount new challenges and apply those victories and insights to other areas. For example, the confidence I gained fighting in front of dozens of elite kickboxers later helped melt away my public-speaking jitters. I would never have guessed those two things were interconnected, but they were.

After my Muay Thai training experience I said to myself, *If you can fight in front of some of the world's greatest fighters, how in the hell can you not speak in front of people? After all, it's only speaking.* As strange as it might sound, learning to box in Thailand transformed my communication confidence—an essential skill for any would-be entrepreneur or CEO.

Likewise, the art of strategic hand-to-hand combat was not unlike the lessons I was learning in my business classes about negotiations and contract disputes. One move affects those that follow; it's all strategy. No matter what happens or how hard you are hit (literally or figuratively), you must always make an effort to keep your mind clear and balanced. Everything is interconnected if you take the time to look close enough.

Some of my favourite times at the camp took place between sparring sessions and the five-mile sprints. Hearing accomplished fighters share stories was a real treat for us less-experienced guys. Without question, the man who taught me the most was Apidej. Embarrassingly, I'd known next to nothing about him when I arrived. He was more than thrice my age. Early on he invited me to grab a beer with him. 'Thank you, but I really need to train and focus,' I told him. (What an idiot I was; I didn't know I was talking to the Fighter of the Century.) He just smiled and went on his way.

Thankfully, after I realized the error of my ways, Apidej was gracious enough to give me more of his time. I treasure the moments he spent with me and the lessons he imparted. One of the more unforgettable of these conversations was the time we discussed the most sensitive issue of his career: the times he'd killed men in the ring.

'How do you feel about it?' I asked him.

'I'm ashamed for what I did' he said with a sombre expression across his face.

'But they knew your power going in; you were known as the strongest kicker in the world. You broke people with one kick.'

'No. I'm very ashamed,' he said trailing off.

It seemed like he might not be done speaking; I remained quiet.

'Five people's lives ended because of me. They had families. I feel deep sadness. Regret.'

I shall never forget those words.

This entire world was new and fascinating to me. The Muay Thai fighters I encountered seemed to live by a unique code of honour and respect—both for themselves and their opponents. The kickboxer's operating credo: pain builds power. These men revered and relished other fighters' skills. Through that admiration for other boxers' talents, they refined their own.

Part of that refinement involved not just fighting tactics but psychological warfare as well. I remember one time I was fighting with a training partner while Apidej looked on. Several minutes into the match, he pulled me aside.

'You're doing good. But why are you showing your emotions on your face?' he asked.

I wiped the sweat off my forehead while maintaining eye contact with my teacher.

'You're showing that you're in pain. Never do that. Because then the other fighter knows he's beating you. Understand?'

I nodded.

'You should smile and laugh when you get kicked or punched.'

'Wait, so when I get punched and kicked by the other fighter, I'm supposed to laugh and smile?' I asked

'Yes' he said. 'Be balanced in your mind. Smile. Laugh. That's the mindset of a champion fighter.'

All these learnings—respect your opponent's abilities, prepare to the hilt, invite pain to build power, master the art of psychological warfare, study the moves of those who've mastered the game—made a lasting impression on me. Even back then I sensed that the application of these lessons might extend beyond fighting. That they would later prove vital to my success in business, I had no idea.

Indeed, during my time in the training camp, all I could focus on was doing my best to keep pace with the other fighters. Once, I did 100 push-ups in a row in front of a couple of guys while we were warming up. They weren't impressed.

'Why are you wasting your time with such easy exercises?' asked a 6'6" baldheaded pro Muay Thai boxer from Amsterdam. 'That stuff is pointless.'

Again, the mindset of fighting culture was worlds apart from anything I'd seen or experienced before. At one point, after a painful defeat during a match, my roommate, now bruised and embarrassed, got down on his knees and touched the camp owner's feet—a cultural sign of supreme respect and total humility. 'I'm so sorry I lost. I embarrassed you. I embarrassed my trainers. I ask your forgiveness.'

The camp owner and trainers had 'invested' in the fighter, but he failed to achieve optimal results. His solemnity and contrition made for a powerful moment I've never forgotten.

At night, when we were getting ready for bed, I would sit on the top bunk bed and look down as my roommate sat on the floor thumbing the bruises on his body. Then the room would fill with the pungent odor of Tiger Balm as he slathered the salve over his wounds. As much as they might hurt, he knew that in the breaking and healing he'd grow stronger.

I was no stranger to injuries and pain either. At one point, I had to be rushed to the hospital to receive an injection when I shredded the joint in my left knee. (When I do certain exercises today, I can still feel that pain in my left leg—a physical 'souvenir' from my boxing-camp experience). But on most nights, like my roommate, I let the pain settle by covering myself with Tiger Balm before lying on the floor writhing for hours. So much of pain management is in the mind. What Apidej taught me was that fighting was more mental than physical. The culture of the camp was to tell yourself that pain was a non-factor; train your brain to say, 'Something hurts? So what? Continue. Keep going.'

To a lay person that might sound crazy or even dangerous. But to fighters it was crazy and dangerous *not* to think that way. For them, their lives were on the line every time they fought. That's why most said a solemn prayer before they got into the ring. It was no joke.

Put simply, recognizing pain was dangerous, both physically and mentally. Without conditioning their minds to ignore pain, they ran the risk of slowing down their reflexes and ability to defend and attack under extreme duress. And in that nanosecond—in that moment of allowing their body to recognize its own aches and agony—an opponent's elbow to the neck could catch them off guard and leave them paralysed or worse. Every match was do or die; they didn't know if they were coming home in one piece or a coffin. So they prepared like every fight might be their last.

Observing this extreme culture and mindset made an indelible mark on me. *What if you treated business like that, like its life or death?* I thought. *How much more would you prepare? How much more would you focus?*

As a college kid studying at an Ivy League business school, I'd uttered many of the same kinds of statements as my fellow students. 'We're working so hard! We're really pushing ourselves! I'm only on two hours of sleep because I was studying all night for an exam!'

Now, lying nightly on the floor of my boxing camp bedroom feeling waves of pain undulate through my body in a fog of menthol-smelling muscle ointment, I realized I had no clue what I was talking about as a complaining college kid. Living with fighters for a summer taught me what pushing yourself truly means. Sure, I'd pushed myself to do 1,000 push-ups, hit the gym for two hours a day, study, and go from a lacklustre student to sitting at the top of the heap. But the boxing camp was a different galaxy of intensity. And although I didn't know it then, certain periods in professional life, such as turnaround businesses, require spurts of extreme passion and intensity. You have to pick yourself and propel yourself forward with a thick skin. The mental, the physical … like I said, it's all connected.

That was one of the most unexpected and valuable surprises: something as seemingly unrelated to business as a boxing camp had left me with insights that proved surprisingly applicable to doing corporate battle. I learned the importance of making an effort to keep the mind as clear and balanced as possible no matter what. Apidej's lesson about not showing pain applied to opponents. But it also applies to yourself, because the more you express, the more you feel.

Another core takeaway was the importance of lateral versus linear thinking. The experience of fighting in public helped me overcome my self-consciousness about public speaking probably more than if I practised public speaking. My tolerance for business risk, complexity, and conflict increased following the fighting experiences as well. In turn, I was able to go into future business ventures with less fear and more confidence, despite all the challenges I would face. Bottom line: when you're up against a major obstacle in any field of life, applying lateral thinking can often open up pathways that lead to unexpected solutions.

Part of devising winning business solutions involves understanding the value of strategy and how it can overcome deficiencies in capabilities—something the boxing camp taught me in dramatic, bone-crushing detail. Despite lesser capabilities, by applying strategic thinking, I'd been able to tie a professional fighter who by all accounts should have wiped the floor with me. But by utilizing things like height and reach differentials and angles of attack, I was able to neutralize his strengths. The application of this concept to business is limitless. And it would become one of my hallmark approaches to turning around companies.

Finally, the camp had shown me that limits are illusions, humility is essential, and understanding people from diverse backgrounds and experiences enhances your capacity for business leadership. The limits others impose on people are not real. If they were, there would have been no way I would have survived and thrived at the camp. Likewise, in business, work ethic, intensity, and resilience whisk away the mythological limits others put in your path like a fan blowing away a cloud of smoke. Even still, it's critical that as one gains confidence pushing past illusory barriers, one still remains a humble business leader. If the greatest fighters in the world can be humble, so can you!

Part of that humility comes from working with diverse groups of people. As an entrepreneur you need to be able work well with people from all types of backgrounds. More than that, you have to understand how to lead and inspire people of all kinds. The boxing camp gave me exposure to people from backgrounds I might not otherwise have encountered. I'm grateful it did. Gaining understanding into others and learning to communicate effectively with people of all kinds is at the heart of business leadership.

As my time inside the camp drew to a close, I made an extra effort to spend any fleeting moments around Apidej and Wooden Man to soak up their wisdom and share my appreciation for all the time and teachings they had poured into a novice boxer like me. I was profoundly grateful. They had both taught me much more than how to execute an elbow thrust or an upper cut. They had created a pure environment, one where they imparted lessons that helped steel our sense of toughness and refined our character.

The day I left, Apidej took me aside and looked me straight in the eye. 'You have a brilliant mind,' he said. 'Use it for good.'

He then knelt down in front of me, touched my feet, and prayed over me. I was shocked and embarrassed. Why was the Fighter of the Century prostrating himself before a college kid with marginal boxing skills? His act of modesty and humility was itself a lesson, one that endures for me even to this day.

As I gathered my things to leave, Wooden Man said he would drop me off at the airport. I rode on the back of a truck. We had formed a strong bond; leaving and saying goodbye was sad for me. When we arrived, I hopped off the truck.

'I can't thank you enough for all you've done for me,' I said. 'I appreciate everything so much. Thank you.'

He smiled and looked at me silently through moist eyes for what felt like a minute. We both knew we would never see each other again. Our lives had intersected for a brief moment in time, one where we'd enjoyed camaraderie through mutual suffering and extreme physical exertion. I was grateful to have met and learned from him along my journey.

Walking into the airport, I looked back over my shoulder. Wooden Man smiled before I waved a final time. Once inside, I headed for a restroom before checking in for my flight. I stood at the sink and looked in the mirror for the first time in months. I hadn't shaved the entire time I'd been at the camp and looked like a bedraggled mess. For some reason the sight of myself with a ragged beard made me chuckle.

As I boarded the flight, my body still radiated pain. Oddly, I had never felt more energized, refreshed, and ready to chase my dreams.

4

Captain a Rowboat Before a Ship, a Ship Before a Fleet

AFTER A SERIES of whirlwind flights from Thailand back home to my college apartment in Pennsylvania, I was jetlagged. I slid my key into the lock, flung open the door, dropped my bags, stumbled my way to the bedroom, and collapsed onto the mattress. I was right back where I'd began the moment I had my epiphany. Only now I had actually done something about it.

Looking up at the ceiling, my mind cloudy from sleep deprivation, a wave of contentment washed over me. In this process, I'd discovered things about myself I never knew and had a renewed sense of clarity and confidence in mind and body, beyond what I had hoped for.

Best of all, after having my ass kicked for a few months, I was ready to kick some ass myself.

I was eager to hit the ground running and apply my reinvigorated sense of intensity and focus. It was time to get to work and do this thing called entrepreneurship. Initially, I found some of Wharton classes overly theoretical. Theory is important; you can learn a lot from reviewing business case studies. But entrepreneurs itch for the practical, roll-up-your-sleeves type of knowledge that comes through *doing*. So when one of my professors, Eric Siegel, announced that we would be partnering up with a classmate to consult a local Philadelphia growth company for a semester-long project, I was excited.

Professor Siegel had been a high-level consultant to major corporations. I loved his practical teaching style backed up with real world advice and knowledge. He told the class that we would get to know our assigned company's owner, learn about the business from the inside out, meet with its key executives and employees, interview industry leaders in its sector, and then provide a comprehensive set of recommendations for how the company could improve. I couldn't wait to get started!

As with all team-based projects, I knew choosing the right partner was half the battle won. I'd made several friends on campus. The diverse student body also included many Indian students, which I found refreshing. Most of the friendships I made weren't necessarily Indian–Americans; rather, students who lived in India and planned to return home after graduation. Unfortunately, none of the people I'd met were in Professor Siegel's class.

The following day, I got an email from a person I'd never heard of before named Kunal Bahl. The short message said something to the effect of, 'Hi, Jason. We haven't met before, but I noticed you made some very insightful points in our last class and would like to be your partner on the consulting project for this class.' The email was friendly enough, but I wanted to make sure this Kunal person would be a partner who was willing to pull his own weight and tackle an equal share of the workload. So I began asking around.

A bunch of the other students from India assured me Kunal was a hard worker and extremely studious. 'Oh that guy, Kunal? He's always studying until 3 a.m. He's a total nerd. You'll like him,' one person told me. Still, I wasn't 100 per cent sure. So I replied asking my mysterious emailer to please send me his resumé. (How nerdy is that?) Kunal graciously sidestepped the formality of a resumé submission and suggested a meeting instead.

Kunal and I hit it off right away. He was a foodie and so was I. We also shared a similar sense of humour. Most importantly, unlike many of our classmates, we possessed a mutual passion for entrepreneurship. While others had an interest in specializing in things like finance or management, Kunal and I wanted to innovate and create. We became the closest of friends. I never imagined what that random email would one day lead to. But back then, Kunal and I were focused on Professor Siegel's growth company consulting project.

The whole thing was a blast. None of it felt like 'work'. We were learning by doing. Best of all, we were studying business from every angle and gaining practical entrepreneurial insights along the way.

After the semester was over, Kunal and I decided we didn't want to wait until graduation to launch a business idea. Why not do something together? Kunal then explained that he had a start-up idea.

'What is it?' I asked.

'It's a toilet spray,' Kunal said.

(I'm sure the Hong Kong kids who called me a *bhangi* would have loved the irony).

'Okay,' I said. 'Tell me more about it.'

'Well, this toilet spray can disinfect a toilet seat.'

'The market for that could really be large,' I said. 'It sounds interesting.'

'But that's not all,' said Kunal. 'It also can warm the seat and emits a pleasant fragrance.'

We got right to work on our big toilet-bowl dream. Like good little business school students, Kunal and I analysed the addressable market, assessed what kind of margin we could get on this type of product, and analysed potential market penetration. We were set to save the world, one disinfected toilet bowl at a time. We called our creation 'SprayIt'.

'This could be a really big business!' I said.

According to the business theories our classes taught us, we were supposed to have some type of sustainable competitive advantage. So we did a lot of research and discovered that Gillette had a patented shaving cream technology that warms and also has a fragrance. We consulted an intellectual property (IP) lawyer. If we tweaked Gillette's creation and added a disinfectant—*voila!*—we could file our own provisional patent using the same technology. Soon we'd be on our way to becoming toilet-bowl billionaires!

'Oh, look at the math, it's so clear,' we told each other. 'We can build an empire off of this!'

We decided to unveil our gift to the universe at the upcoming Penn Invention entrepreneurship competition—a joint event between UPenn's engineering and business schools. We filled out the application, created the required business plan, and began preparing for our big presentation in front of the judging committee.

There was just one problem: we didn't have the money to build the product or a prototype. Not to fear! We devised a solution: we would pay some kid majoring in animation $50 to create a 3-D computer video of a SprayIt aerosol can squirting liquid on a toilet with little flowers wafting up from the seat.

The evening before the big event, Kunal and I stayed up the entire night slurping down pots of coffee as we rehearsed and perfected our SprayIt presentation. The next day, one of my beloved Wharton mentors, Professor Lawrence Gelburd, who taught the main entrepreneurship class, graciously showed up and sat in the audience to lend us moral support.

The moment had arrived. We took the stage before a throng of fifty or so to unleash our toilet-bowl revolution. A few minutes in as our 3-D animation began, I looked out into the audience at Professor Gelburd. He put his hand on his forehead and looked down as if to say, 'Oh dear God. This is awful.' *Not to worry*, I thought. *We clearly have the best business plan. So what if other competitors may have actual products and we only have a video of a can spraying a toilet with tiny flowers and a glowing seat? We've got this in the bag!*

The judges had made their final decisions. It was now time to award the winners.

First place: an actual, functioning, field-tested robot that defuses landmines to save countless human lives.

Second place: a path-breaking hip-replacement product that had already been created and tested, and was projected to revolutionize the field of medicine.

And coming in third place: SprayIt, some nonexistent thing—but with an animation!—of a mythical product you slather on your toilet seat that warms your butt!

Needless to say, our first dip into the ocean of entrepreneurship was a humbling experience.

(I mean really ... who cares about some dumb robot and hip replacement that will save humanity ... everyone needs a SprayIt ... come on!)

In all seriousness, our first foray into entrepreneurship taught us so much about the holistic nature of starting a business from scratch. Being creative, analysing legal aspects, addressing consumer needs, creating a marketing plan, measuring margins, researching technology—our little SprayIt experiment had served us well by teaching us basic, core start-up principles.

Kunal and I didn't continue to pursue SprayIt (the IP protection challenges were many). But the experience had shown us the exciting freedoms that come with entrepreneurship. It offered more control over your own destiny, who you worked with, what you worked on, and limitless creativity to apply to the multidimensional nature of business, including consumer research, product design, intellectual property protection, marketing, sales, and financial projections.

And that third-place finish also served up a heaping dose of humility (never a bad thing). Kunal and I still laugh about it to this day.

The entrepreneur competition stoked the fire in my belly for the rush that comes from getting your hands dirty and doing the real work of business. Now I wanted more.

Then one day at Wharton I was in my corporate finance class when the professor taught us about US bankruptcy laws. According to our instructor, in America there was something called Chapter 11 bankruptcy and another type called Chapter 7 bankruptcy. I'd taken down the notes and studied the reading assignment on the topic but hadn't thought much more about it. Shortly thereafter, Dinesh called me. The subject of our favourite comic book company—Valiant—came up.

'Hey, remember that company Acclaim Entertainment that bought Valiant?'

'Yeah, what about them?'

'Well, turns out they're actually in bankruptcy.'

'Wow. Really? What kind of bankruptcy?'

He wasn't sure.

'I'll look it up and try to find out. But Dinesh, if it's Chapter 7, according to my corporate finance class, they will have to liquidate everything. Like literally the furniture in the office. And if that happens, they will have to liquidate Valiant.'

We both were silent for a moment.

'What an amazing opportunity to try and bid to buy Valiant!'

As soon as the topic of a Valiant bankruptcy sale arose, one number began glowing in my mind: $65,000,000. That's how much money Acclaim Entertainment paid in 1994 to purchase Valiant comics.

The notion that two penniless college kids could swoop down in 2005 and buy up their favourite childhood comic book company in a bankruptcy fire sale was so outlandishly absurd, so patently audacious that it's incredible Dinesh and I even allowed ourselves to dream such a thing, let alone attempt it. But that's exactly what we were about to do.

At Wharton I had studied the Marvel turnaround case study that Harvard Business School published. Education is extremely valuable; you never know when and where your classroom learnings will manifest. Still, there were massive headwinds arrayed against us. For starters, Valiant had amassed a catalogue of over 1,500 comic-book characters. Beyond my favourites like Harbinger, Shadowman, and Eternal Warrior, there were others with a strong fan base, such as Bloodshot, Ninjak, Rai, Archer & Armstrong, and X-O Manowar.

A trove of intellectual property that rich was bound to go for a bundle—even if the company was in bankruptcy.

Second, heavy hitters like Marvel's Jim Shooter and Bob Layton—some of my creative idols growing up—had put Valiant on the map in the early 1990s before Acclaim Entertainment came in and screwed things up. That meant big-time players with deep pockets, such as Marvel, DC Comics, Disney, and others, were likely to acquire the Valiant universe.

Third, even if these corporations never did anything with the characters, they would be clearing the field of future competition. Put another way, swiping the Valiant chess piece off the industry playing board made strategic business sense. Or, if they wanted to make a mint, they could utilize their massive budgets and brand power to relaunch Valiant characters into the stratosphere. Either way, the top dogs were almost sure to beat out other bidders.

And finally, the odds of two college kids with no cash, no experience, and no industry knowledge going up against wealthy corporate titans or industry insiders with armies of expensive lawyers were next to nil. We were so naïve and green, we didn't even know how a bankruptcy auction worked, nor the vast and complex legal minefield one must tap dance through during the process. But where there is challenge, there is also opportunity. Those who chose to do hard things—the actions few others are willing to take—gain the rewards others miss out on.

The one thing we did know was this: as kids, Valiant characters had captured our hearts and minds. Those stories meant so much to us, and they'd helped get us through our awkward adolescent years. To now let them fall into the hands of an unfeeling corporation that might toss them in the shredder or lock them away in a vault felt like betraying and abandoning one's friends. Plus, depending on the bankruptcy purchase price, we knew acquiring a media property like Valiant could be a once-in-a-lifetime opportunity.

'Of course, 99 per cent we will not be successful,' I remember telling people when we first started flirting with the idea. 'Someone like Disney will see the wisdom in buying these assets and will grab them. But I will always regret it if I don't at least try. There's no way we will get this, but I need to give it my all or I'll never forgive myself.'

So, that's what I did.

With Dinesh studying film out on the West Coast in California, and me back east in Philadelphia studying business, I used my Wharton classes as an information gathering resource. I needed to quickly learn as much as I could about a Chapter 7 bankruptcy and what happens when a company liquidates itself through an auction. My ignorance was almost comical. I would literally thumb through my business school textbooks looking for answers to questions. Fortunately, I was blessed with gracious Wharton professors who entertained my novice inquiries and helped explain how a bankruptcy sale works. I then relayed my learnings to Dinesh as we had fun pursuing our fantasy of possibly bidding in the Valiant auction.

Had either of us really understood how mind-numbingly complex and riddled with setbacks, headaches, and heartbreaks our entrepreneurial adventure was going to be, I wonder if we would have ever embarked on that journey. Untangling IP rights, deciphering contracts, tracking down vital missing corporate documents strewn across the US, raising capital, fighting and winning legal battles, hiring and managing a team, learning what it means to run a company and make a payroll—we had to learn how to captain a row boat before we could steer a ship or lead a fleet.

Thankfully, our youthful ignorance allowed us to forge ahead and pursue a media property that we were convinced could one day stand on the world stage alongside the likes of a Marvel or DC Comics.

The treasure hunt of our lives had officially begun.

The first thing I learned about the bankruptcy auction process was that the assets for sale were not packaged or marketed well. That's putting it mildly. Instead of a traditional, organized business deal where things are listed out clearly on a deal sheet, this was more like searching for a diamond inside the dusty, disorganized stockroom of an abandoned *kirana* (the neighbourhood grocery) store that had been hit by a tornado.

The process worked like this. First, a company would place an obscure advert in a newspaper announcing to come to such and such courtroom on such and such date to bid on asset X. Beyond that, you were pretty much on your own. What exactly you were buying, and whether there were strings attached to it, was unclear. It was up to you the bidder to do proper due diligence or face the consequences.

I wrote a letter to the trustees of the bankruptcy in an attempt to speak with the attorneys in charge of the auction. No response. Then I found a lawyer who allegedly knew the attorneys and had him reach out. Still no response. I asked him to keep contacting them. Again and again he tried. Finally, after several attempts, we got ahold of the lawyers running the auction. 'Can we please take a look at the Valiant assets so we know what we're bidding on?' we asked.

'Sure. The papers are in a warehouse on the outskirts of Long Island,' they told us. 'You look through those and figure out what's there and what's not and you bid on it.' Their basic attitude towards the auction's contents was: *You decipher which comic-book characters you would own, those you wouldn't, and those you might only own partially. We don't know, we don't care, you figure it out.*

I'd never been to this part of Long Island, New York, and was unsure how safe the area was. The warehouse was about a three-hour drive from the Wharton campus, but I didn't own a car. So I took a train to the area and grabbed a cab to the actual location.

I also decided to bring a lawyer with me to help interpret whatever legal papers I might encounter. I'd convinced my father to grant me a small loan to cover legal expenses to determine whether bidding on Valiant was even possible. My pitch: 'This company used to be worth $65 million. Now maybe it can be bought for next to nothing!'

I'm not sure what I was expecting, but a dusty warehouse roughly the size of a basketball court plunked down in the middle of nowhere wasn't it. When the cab rolled up to the shady-looking building, I questioned whether we were in the right place.

Other than the two cars in the parking lot, the place looked abandoned. My lawyer and I stepped out of the cab and walked towards the lonely structure. I opened the door. There, waiting inside, was a warehouse worker and someone from the trustee lawyer's firm to babysit us and make sure we didn't steal documents. They walked us to a row of shelves.

'These two rows are related to the materials you're interested in,' the warehouse worker said.

I looked down the length of the aisles. Dozens of old cardboard boxes were strewn about in no discernible order. I guess I'd assumed there would be filing cabinets with organized, tabbed folders. To the contrary, this was more like a junk shop. It was as if there had been a massive fire at the Valiant offices and people had grabbed stacks of paper off their desks and tossed them into random boxes. I raised an eyebrow at my lawyer.

'Alright then,' I said. 'I guess we'll start at one end and work our way down.'

I still remember lifting the lid off that first cardboard box. Valiant was the company that fuelled my childhood passion for comics. I was the same geek who, as a teenage assistant to Jackie Chan, was more mesmerized by media-distribution contracts. Now, sitting in that dusty warehouse, I was about to pull back the curtain and get a behind-the-scenes peek into Valiant's inner sanctum. When I thumbed through the papers inside that first box, I felt like I was looking at sacred, magical documents. Memos between comic creators, company agreements, articles of incorporation, a potential deal to turn a character into a toy, cool original artwork and character sketches—I was in fanboy heaven.

After spending over a half-hour sifting through that first box in a trance, I snapped myself to attention by reminding myself why I was there in the first place. I needed to understand exactly what assets this auction was offering for sale. For example, were all 1,500 comic-book characters owned by Valiant? Or did artists and writers hold the intellectual property rights for certain creations? And if the latter, what kind of terms or profit-sharing agreements were in place between Valiant and the artists responsible for creating a character?

These questions and scores more like them had to be ironed out in advance. Without reconstructing clear chains of title, there would be no legitimate way to do a movie deal or a merchandise deal with a character. I knew enough from my business classes that I couldn't just say, 'Hey, we own this character. Trust us.' Any effort to monetize a character would first need proof that we owned the rights. Without those documents, no entertainment company or toy manufacturer's legal department would approve future deals.

Riffling through those initial boxes, two things became crystal clear. First, attempting to determine clear chains of title for the entire Valiant universe of characters amid these dozens of messy boxes was going to require many, many trips back to the warehouse. And second, it occurred to me that key papers might not be in the boxes at all. That would mean we wouldn't even be able to establish clear ownership over characters. If that were the case, the auction wouldn't so much be for the sale of Valiant as a company; rather, it would be more like buying stacks of cool drawings for a private art collection. The difference was vast. One could yield an empire, the other a modest eBay auction to unload old memorabilia.

After a few hours, my lawyer and I called a cab to come pick us up. We chatted on the car ride back to the train station.

'Well,' he said, 'what do you think? A little overwhelming, isn't it?'

'You know, it's funny,' I replied. 'I know untangling all of this is going to be a big, complicated process. But I want to keep ploughing through it. I really believe this could be a once-in-a-lifetime opportunity. Everything back there was a mess. And I'm sure people with lots of money are probably looking at these materials as well. But I want to keep digging and see this thing through. One man's trash is another man's treasure.'

He nodded and smiled the way a parent might at a naïve child.

Had I not been so passionate about Valiant's comic-book characters, or believed that it could become a major superhero entertainment company, there's no way I would have had the fire in the belly necessary to keep going after that first trip to the warehouse. This was going to be a daunting gauntlet—one fraught with hidden pitfalls and invisible legal trapdoors that could unlatch at a moment's notice, hurtling us into a financial freefall. But something inside me just wouldn't let go. To my core, I believed this adventure was a risk worth taking.

When I got back to Wharton, I called Dinesh to debrief him on my first trip to the warehouse. I didn't sugarcoat the reality: performing proper due diligence was going to be like solving a Sherlock Holmes detective case. Still, I knew this was my chance to make something of my life. I had finally turned my personal life around. And I now knew myself well enough to know that I was an entrepreneur at heart. I was also an immigrant in the US who had been blessed to attend a great school. It was now or never.

Over the next four months, I made no less than ten trips to warehouses. I say warehouses, plural, because what I soon discovered was that Valiant's papers were strewn across America in other locations as well. Dinesh made the trip out from his college campus in California and joined me on a few of those document digs. We couldn't afford to have the lawyer with us each time, so we went alone and took thorough notes.

Juggling college coursework with the frequent warehouse expeditions was exhausting. When we weren't travelling, we were conducting online research and making dozens of cold calls to anyone and everyone previously connected to Valiant. Our goal was to piece together as much information as possible before the auction courtroom showdown.

Our greatest fear was missing documents. The auction would be on an 'As is, where is' basis. That meant you could bid on the asset, win, and later discover your winnings lacked key agreements that might significantly diminish the asset's value. One of our most serious concerns was that there might be a document tucked away in some unknown cardboard box somewhere that declared that Valiant had licensed all its film rights to Disney or someone else.

So we made an extra effort to crosscheck the documents we had seen in the warehouse boxes with industry people and online announcements of things like the sale or licensing of film rights, television rights, or product rights. If, for example, we read press announcements for a movie deal for Eternal Warrior, but hadn't located them in the warehouse files, we knew to flag it and assume that Eternal Warrior film rights were missing.

To say it was a complex 1,500-piece puzzle is an understatement. We were burning the candle at both ends, messaging and calling each other back and forth from our respective college campuses. Any spare minute I wasn't in class was spent drilling down into Valiant. *Whatever it takes*—that was my operating mindset.

During our search we heard a rumour that a former Marvel executive was vying to grab Valiant for a ridiculously low price of something like $75,000. Initially, we worried that we might have missed out on the bargain of the century. But later we learned that a deal had not, in fact, been brokered; the $75,000 figure was merely what's known as a 'stalking horse'—a low-end bid on a bankrupt company's assets.

Still, we knew others were definitely sniffing around. Even if a behemoth like Disney stayed on the sidelines, there was DC Comics, Marvel, and other industry players like Dark Horse and Image who knew Valiant's value and might show up at the courtroom auction.

The process was intimidating. We lacked business knowledge of the industry. Other than trading and selling comic books as kids, we'd never worked in the market. We didn't have any connections to artists or writers. And we sure as heck didn't have any money. Self-doubt crept in. *Who are you kidding, Jason? These are serious, wealthy industry professionals. You're a college kid who can barely scrape enough money to visit warehouses and cover legal fees. You have to comb through your business textbooks and search online to even understand what basic bankruptcy terms mean.*

Whenever these thoughts arose, I centred my mind on a simple truth: *This is a once-in-a-lifetime chance—an entrepreneurial opportunity that could forever change the lives of you and your family. Just give it your very best shot. Then you'll be able to sleep well at night knowing you gave it your all.*

During our months of digging we discovered that a major film studio did, in fact, have a deal for one of the key Valiant characters.

There were also three other characters—Solar, Magnus, and Turok—that had licensing deals. Beyond those four, however, our research led us to believe that all other Valiant characters should be included in the sale unencumbered, without any hidden strings attached.

With the date of the courtroom bankruptcy auction nearing, and with our months of sleuthing concluded, it was now time for Dinesh and me to talk money—or the lack of it thereof.

We had no idea how much Valiant might go for at auction. We asked others for their opinions to get a range of figures. The rules of the auction allowed the winner no less than sixty days before they had to pay the bank to close the deal. Still, we needed to agree on a ceiling price above which we would not go. We also needed to figure out how we would come up with the cash in the unlikely event we actually won at auction.

Dinesh and I determined that the highest we would bid was roughly $600,000. Even saying a number like that out loud felt insane. As college kids, neither of us had any personal funds to contribute. That meant we would each be responsible for somehow raising $300,000.

We didn't get all the money in hand before the auction, because the odds were stacked against us winning. Still, we needed to begin lining up friends and family for soft commitments to provide some degree of assurance that we could raise the capital to cover the purchase if, by some miracle, we won. By hook or by crook, we were determined to do whatever it took to secure the funds should they be necessary to clinch the deal.

Our primary investor pitch to friends and family was that these were real assets that had previously been worth $65,000,000. We explained that the business case was so strong that even if we simply packaged and marketed the assets better, we could flip them for resale and turn a handsome profit. I was convinced this argument was true. Having spent months sifting through reams of disorganized papers trying to deduce trademark and licensing rights made me certain that the Valiant property could be sold for a sizable sum even if we reorganized the materials and presented their value in a clear, objective, and measurable way.

One rule of thumb on valuing IP is how large is the awareness of the assets and how strong is the emotional connection to the IP. In Valiant's case, it was strong for both. The company had previously sold eighty million comic books and eight million video games based on its characters. In addition, it had a raving fan base. They don't call people 'fans'—short for 'fanatics'—for nothing. People had created their own Valiant clothes and toys. Some had even gotten Valiant characters tattooed on their bodies. And two fans were so extreme in their devotion to Valiant that they were now trying to buy the company!

We rounded out our pitch for capital with the caveat that us winning was highly unlikely but that if we did, investors would be getting in on the ground floor of a company that industry publications once called the next Marvel—a media empire already valued in the billions. I pitched each conversation the same way: 'The odds are against it coming to fruition. But if by some chance it does, and we win this, it will change all our lives forever.'

Our families and friends were encouraging and receptive. We were extremely grateful for their nurturing responses and verbal commitments of support. It was a much-needed confidence booster heading into our courtroom auction battle in New York.

With the semester winding down, ironically, I was busy preparing for a final group presentation for my entrepreneurship class. My studies had taken a hit from all the travelling back and forth to warehouses.

But I justified it in my mind. *It's worth it*, I told myself. *Besides, you're learning entrepreneurship hands-on.*

The night before the auction, three other members of our four-person group and I stayed awake all night working on our class project.

'Guys, I'm really sorry. But I've got to get going to grab a train to New York,' I told them at 6 a.m.

Dinesh and I met in New York. I'd never been to a courtroom before. I wore my cheap, ill-fitting suit. We looked like the college kids we were. Were it not for the fact that we had brought along an IP lawyer and a bankruptcy attorney, I'm not sure anyone would have taken us seriously.

We wanted to get to the building early to scope out the place and size up the competition to figure out who was who. A group of men had arrived in a limousine. Then another man walked into the courtroom wearing the fanciest, most expensive-looking watch either of us had ever seen.

'Did you see that guy's watch?' Dinesh whispered to me.

I nodded.

'Is that guy from Disney?', I whispered back, pointing at one of the men who had arrived by limo.

'I don't know,' he said softly. 'I'm not sure.'

We had no idea where these guys were from but they all looked rich.

The time had finally arrived. The auction began.

Bidding started at $75,000.

I bid a few thousand dollars higher.

The guy with the fancy watch, who turned out to be the former chairman of Acclaim, started bidding as well.

I raised the number another few thousand.

He countered.

I bid again, being careful to only raise the amount no more than $2,000 at a time, so as to inch the number up slowly to try to get the lowest price.

Suddenly, out of nowhere, the fancy watch dude from Acclaim dropped the hammer and started bidding in $50,000 increments.

'What the hell just happened?!' I whispered to Dinesh.

'Hold on,' I said to our lawyers. 'Can we take a break?' They made the request and bought us some time.

Dinesh and I huddled with our advisers, 'What is going on here?'

'It's an intimidation tactic. They're showing you they're not messing around. They're trying to scare you off by showing they have deep pockets.'

Dinesh and I decided we were still in. We reconfirmed that $600,000 was our limit. The bidding resumed.

We went back and forth with the former Acclaim chairman, watching the number climb higher and higher. So far, we were the only two parties who had placed a bid. Round after round we went.

$300,000 … $400,000 … $500,000 … the number kept rising. When the figure hit $600,000, Dinesh and I said *screw it*—and kept on bidding.

$600,000 … $700,000 … $800,000 … we were treading into deeper and deeper financial waters—depths far beyond our grasp.

You'll just figure out a way to borrow or raise more money, I told myself. *You can't give this up. This is your chance!*

Then, around the $900,000 mark, a man who had yet to bid spoke up.

'$925,000,' he said.

Everyone turned and looked at him. It turned out that he was a former Marvel executive who had been lying in wait the entire time.

Dinesh and I looked at each other. The Marvel bidder had only outbid us by $10,000. But the writing was on the wall. This guy was going to go the distance. Enough was enough. We couldn't do this anymore. We had already blown our bidding cap by nearly a third of a million dollars. I'd conditioned my mind to never quit, never give up. But the math was too clear to ignore. We were outgunned. These were men who wore expensive watches and arrived in limos. The fact that the Marvel bidder came in at the very end signalled he was just getting started. He had the finances to knock us out. So, we did the only thing we could do: we stopped bidding.

The auction was over.

At $925,000, the ex-Marvel executive had officially won the Valiant auction.

Dinesh and I got up from our chairs and walked over to the winner. We shook his hand and congratulated him. On the outside, I was smiling, trying to remain professional and composed. After all this wasn't personal, it was business. But to me it *was* personal. The opportunity of a lifetime—a chance to own the next Marvel—had been within my grasp. I'd spent months researching, analysing, and dreaming about it. But now, just as my fingertips were outstretched to grab the golden rung on the ladder of my dreams, a swinging axe had whooshed in front of me and hacked it off.

In the cab ride with the lawyers, our attorneys tried to lift our spirits. They congratulated us on our efforts and said we should be proud to have come as far as we did. They were right: to even get to this point was beyond where we thought we would get. But to have been so close and still come up short made the sting hurt all the more.

'Yeah, but we got this far and we lost by $10,000!' I said.

That was a lot of money to us. But there was no escaping the feeling that we'd just allowed the biggest opportunity of our lives to slip through our hands. I remember wondering whether I'd ever come across a better business deal in my life. I had let myself dream the big dream: to imagine myself as co-owner of the company that produced my favourite childhood comics. I'd envisioned us building

Valiant into an entertainment empire—one where we cut deals with major movie studios to turn our comic-book characters into blockbuster films, video games, and toys. But, in the end, just as we knew was likely to happen, an industry insider from a powerhouse like Marvel had swooped in with a bigger bank account and snatched away the Valiant universe and its 1,500 characters. To say we were heartbroken doesn't even begin to capture it.

Later that same day, hours after the auction had ended, Dinesh and I were still reeling from our loss when the phone rang. It was one of our lawyers.

'Guys,' he said, 'something really, really strange has happened.'

5

Money Isn't a Goal, It's a Byproduct

NOTHING COULD HAVE prepared me for the lawyer's next words.

'So the Marvel guy who won the auction is apparently hesitating to close the deal. There's a problem across the entire trademark portfolio,' he said.

'Wait, what? I don't understand,' I replied.

'Yeah, so the word I'm hearing is that it's been leaked to industry media that there's a shell company—something called Valiant Intellectual Properties, LLC—that claims they actually hold the trademarks to the Valiant characters.'

'But we thought you told us that Valiant owns the trademarks, so what's going on here?'

'Well they do own the trademarks, but you see they apparently didn't renew them. The renewal should have happened during the bankruptcy period. But it looks like this company—this, "Valiant Intellectual Properties"—has come in and claims they have the trademarks.'

Dinesh and I looked at one another.

The lawyer continued: 'No one expected anyone to do that, so now this whole thing is a mess. That's why the guy from Marvel who won the auction is getting cold feet about closing the deal.'

'So ... what does this mean exactly?', I asked.

'What it means is that you guys need to figure out what this Valiant Intellectual Properties, LLC thing is, determine if it's legitimate or not, and sort out how strong their legal argument is. You should also find out if they're well-funded.'

'Just to be clear: are you saying we still might have a shot at this?' I asked.

'Unclear. Let's not get ahead of ourselves,' he said. 'Just start digging and see what you can find.'

Having just come off the biggest disappointment of my life to that point, I refused to allow myself to get excited again. There would be no rekindling of wild-eyed visions of entrepreneurial grandeur. Besides, I reasoned, it was probably just some technical glitch that would get sorted out before the auction winner inked the final deal.

Nevertheless, I was curious who was behind this 'Valiant Intellectual Properties, LLC'. It was nothing I'd come across in my warehouse hunts. That annoyed me, actually. Had I not done thorough research? For the next few weeks, I decided to dig in and find out.

By claiming to control the trademarks, the group could potentially squeeze the holder into selling them the assets. It was a backdoor manoeuvre. Whether it would work or not was anyone's guess.

I soon discovered that the lawyer representing the shadowy entity was a graduate of my university. I decided to play the 'fellow alumni' angle and gave him a call. Big mistake. He wasn't having any of it. As soon as I launched into some chummy University of Pennsylvania banter, he shut me down.

'Look, I don't have time to talk about college. Can I help you with something?'

Gulp.

'Uh, yeah … well, my partner and I were bidders on the Valiant assets,' I explained. 'We don't know who your clients are, but they seem to think that they own the trademarks on the characters. So apparently there's been a big misunderstanding.'

'Wrong,' he said tersely. 'There is no misunderstanding. My client owns all these trademarks.'

'Well, can we at least sit down and talk to your client?'

'I don't know if my client is going to meet you or speak to you. I can't disclose who they are. If they want to talk to you, I'll let you know. Now, if you'll excuse me, I've got to go.'

Click.

(So much for collegiate comradery … Go University of Pennsylvania Quakers!)

The call was a rude awakening, but it stoked the fire inside again. The more I dug in, the more I realized how weak their legal argument was. As it turned out, the guy behind the mysterious intellectual property group was from an independent company—not Marvel or DC. By pulling the trademark-renewal stunt, he may have thought he could snag the assets on the cheap.

By now I was back in full Valiant obsession mode. I was convinced the so-called 'Valiant Intellectual Properties, LLC' claims were flimsy at best and could be beaten.

Screw it, I told myself. *We'll buy these assets and fight this shell company in court. They don't have Marvel-size money. Neither do we.*

But we'll figure it out. After all, this is a once-in-a-lifetime opportunity. I'm not going to let these bullies get in our way and screw this up for us.

It was now a race against time. As long as the Marvel auction winner remained skittish and didn't sign off on the deal, there was still a chance we could convince the legal trustee holding the assets to sell them to us instead. But if the auction winner figured out the Valiant Intellectual Properties riddle and still felt comfortable enough to move forward, the assets were his because he won the auction.

I called the trustee. He played coy.

'We heard the deal hasn't closed and that there's a big problem,' I said.

'No, there's not a big problem,' he bluffed.

'Yes, there is—I *know* there's a big problem,' I replied. 'And you and I both know that the auction winner may never close this deal, because of all the mess with the trademarks.'

'Okay,' he said. 'Go on.'

'Well, the assets are technically unsold and still available for purchase. We may be willing to go ahead anyhow and let you sell them to us,' I said, 'but you would have to give us a big discount.'

A price negotiation commenced. The numbers were much bigger than the battle I'd had with the chessboard street vendor as an eight-year-old on the streets of Agra. But, in the end, I got him to shave $200,000 off the original auction price before we settled on $725,000.

Looking back, I realize I could have probably gotten a better price. But I didn't want to risk pushing too far and lose the deal. This was a unique asset; there was no similar opportunity or deal like it. Also, as the saying goes: pigs get fed, hogs get slaughtered. Become greedy and you can kill a negotiation. It's always better to leave a little something on the table for the other person and make it a win-win deal. It's good for long-term business and often the right thing to do.

'If you sign the papers and wire the $725,000, the assets are yours,' he said.

Suddenly this was all real and immediate. Misty, romantic dreams had been whisked away; the cold, hard realities of business were now staring me in the face. I would either secure more money than I had ever imagined or I would lose my shot at owning a piece of Valiant.

Entrepreneurs often say that your first funding is your hardest. That's true in more ways than one. At least it was for me. There is, of course, the obvious—you have no track record. That means you're typically left to turn to friends and family to raise capital. And it is that second part—asking the people you love and care about most to entrust you with the money they've spent years struggling to earn—that is the toughest on your heart.

The gravity of the moment and the risks involved weigh on you, washing over you in a wave of humility and concern. But if you're motivated, and you truly believe in your dream, you can channel and harness that feeling of responsibility and appreciation to develop a mindset that says: *I refuse to fail. Not just in business, but fail the people who believed in me enough to back my goal with their hard-earned resources.*

I'll never forget the conversations I had with my family members when they decided to put up huge portions of their life savings. My father had heard me float enterprising ideas before. Some of them were even good. But he had never seen this level of conviction and tenacity from his son. Valiant held the potential to change all our lives and he knew it. I spent hours answering all of his important questions. Then he spoke words I still remember. 'I trust you, my son. I'm going to help you do this. I will put in money and raise as much as our family can. But Jason, you *really* have to make this work.'

For a man who was often short on compliments, it was the biggest one he could have paid me. His trust shone through in actions, not words. Later, the financial burden this level of trust placed on our family during Valiant's lean early years would strain my relationship with my family for many years. But when it mattered most, they stood firmly by my side. I'm forever grateful.

Dinesh came through with his portion of the funds as well. Wiring that much money on the day of the transaction felt surreal. Then doubts swarmed my brain like a squadron of killer bees.

If this fails, how will we ever face our family and friends who broke their banks for us?

What will we do if we're saddled with all that debt?

Even if we do own Valiant assets ... then what?

I decided to visit my Wharton professor Lawrence Gelburd in the hope his words of congratulation might buck me up and calm me down. Bad move.

'Wait' he said, 'I know you said you raised the funds to acquire the assets. But how much did you and your partner raise in operating capital to run this thing?'

My stomach cinched in a knot.

'Well ... um ...' I muttered.

'Oh my God, Jason. Please tell me you have a war chest to actually run the business, like rent the office space, hire the staff, do the legal work, buy equipment, pay artists ... I mean you're joking, right?'

I felt like I wanted to throw up.

'We raised about $30,000 more dollars than we had to wire. So that's our operating money, I guess.'

'$30,000?! Are you kidding?! How the hell are you going to run a business with that? That's not enough money to do anything! It's certainly not enough to run an entertainment company.'

I wanted to melt into the floor and trickle out under the door.

'Well,' I said softly looking at the floor. 'We'll figure it out. Have to raise more money, I guess.'

Beyond pointing out the gaping money hole staring us in the face, the conversation with my professor had delivered another cold slap in the face. If I'd thought that the hard part was scurrying around in warehouses, learning bankruptcy laws, hustling for legal help, bidding at auction, negotiating with the legal trustee, raising a mountain of money as a college kid, and securing the Valiant comic book assets, I was sorely mistaken.

As I was about to learn, that had all been the easy part. The *real* work had not even begun.

From 2007 to 2013, Valiant Entertainment was my life.

I wish I could tell you that our company shot onto the comic scene like a bullet out of a gun—zooming straight and on-target. But that's not what happened. At all.

Dinesh decided to stay in California and serve as our chief creative officer (CCO). As Valiant's CEO, I felt it was important that I set up shop where all the industry action was located—in New York City, where real estate costs were astronomical. Starting out with no cash flow, I couldn't afford office space. Hiring employees was also out of the question. Still, we knew we needed a seasoned hand to guide us, someone who understood the comic book industry to help shepherd our journey.

I set up meetings with anyone who would take my calls. Many dismissed me as a clueless kid. But one executive—former head of Valiant under Acclaim, Walter Black—gave me the time of day and much, much more.

Walter will forever be a saint in my mind. He was twice my age. What's more, he had real industry experience. Hiring someone with legacy knowledge and relationships is key when entering a well-established market. Better still, because Acclaim had owned Valiant,

Walter knew what had gone wrong and where the real opportunities remained.

After hours of conversation, I convinced Walter that our dream of resuscitating Valiant back to life could become a reality. Even though we had zero money and couldn't pay him a single cent, I said if he helped us start and fought by our side, one day, when we succeeded, I would make it up to him.

To my amazement, Walter agreed. In fact, he did even more. For two solid years, he worked with me in New York City and helped me battle through my bleakest moments—times when it looked like I might have made the biggest mistake of my life.

Since we had no money for an office, Walter took the train into the city and met me at Penn Station (New York City's main subway hub). There, we worked on the tables and benches. No joke. We literally worked out of the train station for a year. When that got tiresome, Walter and I started hopping from restaurant to restaurant. We'd hole up in a corner table and order a Coke or the cheapest item on the menu.

After a few hours, the restaurant staff would get annoyed that I was too cheap (cash-strapped) to order a full meal while tying up table space. So we'd move on to another restaurant and do it all over again. After another year of bouncing from eatery to eatery, we finally decided to make my apartment 'living room' (my couch and a chair) our primary base of operation.

Initially, perhaps because of my business school education, I was fixated on developing the perfect 'business model'. Like a good Wharton grad, I analysed the industry in detail. In school I studied hard to get good grades. Now I was studying because my business and life depended on it. I was desperate to figure out the best way to make the Valiant assets successful. Was it film? Television? Console gaming? Mobile gaming? Consumer products? Traditional comic book publishing? If the latter, should we publish new or classic content? I wasn't sure.

Every conversation with an industry professional I viewed as a sort of mini focus group to get answers to my questions. Comic writers, editors, artists, publishing executives, marketing gurus, licensing experts—no matter the person I spoke to, the goal was to extract as many tidbits of information as possible. Like the frames of a comic book page, each insight filled in a piece of the broader picture of what needed to happen and in which order. But all that was secondary to the most vexing and potentially lethal problem facing our fledgling company. Like a regenerated villain from one of our comic stories, the shell company that had claimed to own the trademarks to the Valiant characters came roaring back with a legal vengeance.

In its simplest form, what happened was that the shell company 'squatted' on the trademarks registered with America's trademark office (something called the US Patent and Trademark Office, or USPTO). Given our shoestring operating budget, we did as much of our own legal work as we could. We contested their trademark applications to the USPTO and explained that the marks had not been renewed because the renewal period was during the bankruptcy.

The shell company launched a delay tactic in response. We hoped it might just be an opening chess move designed to spark a resolution. But it wasn't. Instead, their street-smart lawyer was prepared to deploy excuse after excuse, delay after delay to make our lives a living hell.

Until we resolved the trademarks, Valiant's assets were all but unusable. We felt we would find a way to win, but that was far from assured. The further we waded into the process, the more complex and riddled with setbacks it became. Things got nasty. A party affiliated with organized crime was pressuring me not to go ahead with Valiant and to just sell it to them instead. If I didn't, they said they would be 'gunning for me'. I used the veiled threat as fuel to develop thicker skin. When you have something of potential value, people will try to snatch it from you.

Nothing about this was going to be easy and I knew it. Because the individual behind the shell company was established in the industry, he could place calls to cut us off from access to key players. Meetings suddenly got cancelled without warning. I was told a whisper campaign was afoot 'not to deal with the brown kid'.

Our opponents pulled out all the stops, using every trick to delay and drain us of resources and time. They had launched a war of attrition. And it worked.

Days became weeks.

Weeks became months.

Months became … two years.

That's how long we languished in the trademark desert.

The anxiety it caused felt, at times, unbearable. Many nights I would lie in bed staring at the ceiling for hours. Eventually I learned how to lull my mind to sleep by listening to New York City's unending orchestra of honking cars and revving engines, punctuated by the occasional yell or laugh from late-night street revellers. The anxiety wasn't ours alone.

The longer the trademark war dragged on and prevented us from inking profitable deals, the louder the chorus of complaints from the family and friends who had invested. When my parents looked at the children of their friends, they saw young adults with secure, stable careers. Engineers, doctors, lawyers, bankers, consultants. These individuals held respectable jobs that brought instant honour and a sense of accomplishment to a family's name. That I couldn't offer the same for my parents frustrated me. It did them, too.

'Why don't you just quit?' my mother said. 'You're wasting your life now.' My father agreed. 'If you stop now maybe you can get an entry level job at a company,' he said. 'Then again, they'll ask what you've been doing for the last two years.'

I responded that I would tell employers the truth, that I was pursuing an entrepreneurial opportunity and making a go of it in the entertainment world.

'Well, I don't think they're going to value that,' he said. 'You're in an obscure industry. Son, it's time to join a bank as an analyst or something before it's too late. If you do it now you can still work your way up and potentially have a career.'

My parents weren't the only ones questioning my path. The farther away I got from my Wharton days, and the longer Valiant lingered without a resolution to the trademark impasse, the more awkward conversations with old college friends and acquaintances grew. They had impressive titles and worked at prestigious places like Goldman Sachs and McKinsey & Co.

Me? I worked on my couch trying to salvage a heap of dusty comic-book characters. It was embarrassing.

I'd hit the entrepreneurial doldrums. Some days it was hard to drag myself out of bed and trudge on. What for? Why? It sure wasn't for the money. There was none. In fact, it was worse than having no money. I had *negative* money. The financial waterline was rushing up all around me faster than I could tread. When I let my mind fixate on it, I felt a shortness of breath. That's not bluster. It's the honest truth. Talk to anyone who has ever been massively in debt.

Better yet, look at the number of high-flying executives who turn to dangerous addictions, have broken marriages, or, tragically, commit suicide. Most business books don't talk about such things. It's uncouth, an ugly topic for polite society. But you can't prevent what you refuse to discuss.

I think it's better to be honest with you now at this early stage of your journey than to dangle shiny objects in your face and pretend entrepreneurship is all glitter and rainbows. The 'get-rich-quick' nonsense out there is fool's gold. In fact, it's much worse than that. It's selling people lies.

Here's what I know: if you're only in it for the money, you'll never make it. Money doesn't come unless you have the tenacity to spend years slogging through the muck. If striking it rich is your obsession, you won't have the stomach to make it through the long phase when you're bootstrapping and cash poor.

I need you to pay attention to the next five sentences. *Money isn't a goal, it is a by-product. The goal is solving problems, developing endurance, evolving, and giving customers the services they want, the products they need, and the experiences they crave. That's called value creation. Money flows to value. When you create the latter, you get the former.*

I wish I had known this back during those dreary first couple of years in New York City. There were times when our hopes were raised, only to have them tumble and fall. For example, a financing deal for the company that would have been transformative, unravelled and fell apart at the last minute. I had already assumed it was a done deal and was celebrating in my mind. Big mistake. Also a valuable reminder that the deal isn't done until it's done.

Bottom line: economic hardships and struggles are endemic to the entrepreneurial journey. So, when you are cash poor and the financial stress has your chest in a vice, know that what you're feeling is normal; you're not alone.

Had Dinesh and I worked together in the same location, perhaps all the stress might not have been so bad. Having someone by your side to confide in and blow off steam with helps take the edge off. But for a time, the isolation, combined with being in a city of nine million strangers, made for a lonely existence.

At one point during this period, I tried my hand at searching for a life partner. I created a profile on Shaadi.com and sent out several messages. I got almost no responses. One of the few responses I did receive was from Kanika, a girl from Mumbai living in New York, with a cute photo. However, we had a completely one-sided conversation; she grilled me on what I did for a living and it never got beyond that. I did my best to explain that I was an entrepreneur and gave her some basic business details. She wasn't feeling it. At all. Her response: Don't call me, I'll call you. Fail!

Still, no matter what my relationship status was, the two-year trademark battle would have been gruelling regardless. The ultimate resolution came when we were told that one of the best ways to bolster our trademark argument was to actually publish something.

Walter's background was book publishing, so we decided to publish a Harbinger graphic novel. There was only one problem, because of the unsettled trademark dispute, Diamond, the dominant distributor of comics, wouldn't distribute our products until the issue was resolved. The solution? We'd publish the thing ourselves and sell it online direct to customers.

We got to work. We built a website, secured warehouse space to do our own drop shipping, and cut a deal with a printer. We also used Amazon. The comic-industry press had covered the saga of the 'Valiant versus Valiant' legal battle. So we knew that us publishing something might cause a stir and make a splash. To heighten the intrigue, we decided to create a new Harbinger story that linked back to the classic tale. To pull this off, we engaged the creative force I'd long idolized, the original Harbinger creator, Jim Shooter. This would be Jim's first story in nearly ten years and would feature the most popular Harbinger characters. It was a gamble, but what did we really have to lose?

When we launched the graphic novel, we could hardly believe the response. Even though Harbinger had been dormant for years, amazingly, we sold tens of thousands of copies and hit #1 on the Amazon bestseller list for graphic novels. Best of all, by using the trademark, we strengthened our legal case.

The shell company responded by printing a comic book of their own. That gave us an opening to sue them in federal court, as opposed to being stuck in the USPTO which was going nowhere. Given how hostile the shell company had become, and the smear campaign they were spreading against 'the brown kid', we sprung for a lawyer—one who knew their attorney personally and could hopefully negotiate effectively.

For maximum leverage, I decided to use an asymmetric negotiation tactic. Specifically, I wanted to appear unpredictable to keep the other side on their heels and second-guessing our next move. I then leaked to people close to the other side that this had gotten so nasty and so ugly that I now considered it personal and no longer about business. The implication was that I was so crazy that I was willing to do whatever it took to bankrupt them.

The result of all these combined efforts was that, within two weeks, we came to a resolution. We would pay the shell company tens of thousands of dollars. In return they would transfer their supposed trademarks to us, dissolve their company, and sign an agreement saying that they had exited the Valiant business forever.

Good riddance!

The trademark victory was euphoric. The shackles were off. We were finally free. It was now time to build and battle.

After the success of Jim Shooter's first story for us, I hired him as Editor-in-Chief. Initially, we envisioned building the company around him, but that was a time-wasting mistake for several reasons. For one, things didn't work out. The fit wasn't right. And second, an entrepreneur should never build their company solely around one person, especially someone else. It's too risky. Better to build a strong team to diversify risk and not place the fate of your company in one person's hands. Lesson learned.

Our next battle was with a major film studio, to win back the film rights to one of our characters. After studying a bunch of technical IP contract laws, I stumbled on something thing called an 'executory contract'. It's a fancy term that basically means that both sides must do something before a contract becomes valid. I believed the contract in question was executory and could therefore be nullified. It would be a risky move. We'd essentially be filing a lawsuit against the other party. The absolute last thing we wanted was to get into another protracted legal battle. Still, we decided to pull the trigger.

We sent the film company notice that we thought the contract was executory and that a bankruptcy court was moving to reject it unless they responded within the allotted time period. Then we waited anxiously, counting down the days on the calendar until the response deadline.

Silence. No response.

Then there was, by law, an appeals period. When the minutes on the clock struck past the deadline, we could hardly believe it. The judge deemed the contract rejected. Just like that, something that was worth at least a million dollars was now back in our possession.

Clawing back the rights to a million-dollar character was a major early win for us.

We built on our victory by committing to doing the tedious but critical job of cleaning up the chains of title for other Valiant comic-book characters with missing paperwork. Most of the characters had been created on a work-for-hire basis. But several of the work-for-hire agreements were missing. Without those papers specifying that the rights transferred from the creator to the company, we could get plunked back into a legal quagmire.

So we went back to many of the original artists and writers, told them we'd like them to do some work for us, and then clumsily asked them to sign an affidavit. Each such affidavit clarified that the work they had previously created at Valiant was indeed on a work-for-hire basis. It listed out each of the characters they had created and transferred rights to the company.

The whole thing was awkward and uncomfortable, but thankfully, many of the artists and writers were cool and accommodating about helping us reconstruct the paper trail. For added safety, I befriended Hollywood's go-to-lawyer on all things chain of title, Dennis Angel (yes, that's really his name).

Among industry insiders, Dennis's legal opinions on film rights were golden. He went back over all our characters and wrote up legal opinions to prove we had the legal rights to our comic characters. On top of all that, we also got errors and omissions insurance. Still, even with our legal house now in order, it was unclear to me how to crack the code on the best business model and strategy for us to pursue.

Then something happened. Shortly after getting our legal problems solved we were approached by a division of Virgin Group called Virgin Comics & Animation. The company, which had Richard Branson, spiritual guru Deepak Chopra, and acclaimed director Shekhar Kapur as partners, now wanted to buy Valiant. To sweeten the deal, they were offering us a more than 10x return on our initial investment.

The temptation to sell was strong. Dinesh and I were living the thrifty financial lifestyle of entrepreneurs. Now, with the stroke of a pen, Virgin was offering to make us millionaires.

But I didn't buy Valiant with the vision of flipping it. Instead, my original goals had been creating a company, building skill sets and myself as an asset. If I sold now, I wouldn't have the chance to continue to evolve as an entrepreneur and CEO by progressing to the more mature stages of the lifecycle of a company. Besides, I fervently believed Valiant could generate a much, much higher selling price if we hunkered down and did the hard work. And that's exactly what we did. No sale.

Dinesh's film background and California presence made our entry into Hollywood the logical next step. But if we thought the comic industry was filled with hard-to-crack cliques, that was nothing compared to Hollywood's gated-universe and 'insiders only' culture.

We were desperate to get our toe in the film-industry door. Maybe if we could somehow interest a director in one of our comic characters, we could begin developing movie projects, we surmised. We started hunting for anyone who had the word 'director' beside their name. We were hilariously naïve. I remember a ridiculous meeting where we sat in a coffee shop with some guy.

'So you're a director?' we asked him.

'Yeah,' he said.

'Cool. So tell us about your directing experiences.'

'I directed a music video one time.'

'That's awesome.'

'Yep … so that was cool.'

Annnd ... that was it. That was the extent of his directing experience. But we were so eager to link up with a 'director', we actually contemplated partnering with him.

Maybe he's right for one of our projects, we rationalized. A real 'diamond in the rough'.

In hindsight, it's easy to say, what the hell were we thinking? But back then, we thought having a director—*any* director—attached to a project would get us into the VIP, red carpet world of Hollywood glitz and fame. But there were no shortcuts, no backstage passes to zip us to the front of the line. Instead, we needed to go back to what works—good old-fashioned research and strategy—to make the breakthroughs that mattered.

When I say 'research', I mean that term in the broadest sense possible. The comic book world was quirky, zany, and not the sort of industry that had hundreds of readymade business case studies to learn from. So we did what I consider some of the best type of research: we hustled to get meetings with people smarter than us who knew the business better than we did.

I met with over fifty people working at various companies, departments, and levels to survey their view of the industry and to figure out what worked and didn't. As part of this effort I also set up meetings with people from media, such as film, television, video games, consumer products, and publishing. I was trying to wrap my head around the media and entertainment business from a holistic perspective to gain a top-to-bottom view of how to rebuild a comic IP-based company strategy from scratch.

I remember grabbing breakfast with Joe Perella, the legendary investment banker who previously ran the firm Wasserstein Perella, and now Perella Weinberg. Joe had done some of the largest deals in history and his firm would eventually do a fundraise for Valiant. I tried to move the conversation towards gaining great business advice. Then, in the middle of our meal, Joe looked at me and said, 'Jason, there is only one piece of advice I'm going to give you.' I leaned in to listen. 'Buy real estate by the ocean!' he said with a smile. Later, I took his advice; but at the time I was hoping for something a little more actionable.

And of course, the other crucial meetings were those we had with people who were part of Marvel's incredible turnaround story of going from bankruptcy to $4.5 billion in just ten years. For those sessions I would just set up a meeting, show up, and *listen*. Today, more and more, I'm seeing younger people who haven't developed soft skills, like in-person communication, emotional intelligence, and listening. In fairness, that's not really their fault. Today's social media environment has bred a generation of people who've spent more time staring at their phones than looking into the eyes of a living, breathing human sitting across from them.

For us, though, being in the room for old school, one-on-one meetings made a world of difference. Old hands in the entertainment world have a saying: 'Always take the meeting.' It means you never know whom you will encounter or what deals and opportunities may emerge when you show up and meet people in the flesh. That was certainly true for us.

While listening to Marvel pioneers explain how they turned a floundering company into a media powerhouse, I started to gain a holistic, wide-angle view of why companies like Marvel and DC had been able to scale themselves to soaring heights, whereas others like Wizard, Dark Horse, and others could never break out of the stratosphere.

After extensive, deep research, I discovered the secret. Instead of approaching the business as a comic-book publisher or even as a production company, the key was applying a business model that could generate a scalable IP company. Let me explain.

Let's say a comic book company published a book with licensed IP and it was a big hit. So what? Even if you took that model to television, film, or gaming, you'd only get a small percentage of the upside, because you didn't own the IP. Now let's say you did own the IP and happened to get a hit. Again, who cares? Other than the obvious sequel that might come from it, it doesn't guarantee that the probability of your other projects will be hits, because every project is essentially a new business, with all the underlying risks that come with a fresh venture.

Put simply, you still haven't solved the 'one-hit wonder' problem in the eyes of big-time investors. Therefore, that model is not likely to create a company of significant value, because even with the occasional hit here and there, the actual value of the company doesn't increase dramatically.

The solution? Create a *shared* universe of IPs that are *interlinked* as part of a larger creative canvas. Maybe that means including a cameo appearance by a related character, or grouping characters together to appear alongside one another to create a force-multiplier, such as with DC's *Justice League* featuring Batman, Superman, Wonder Woman, The Flash, Aqua Man, Cyborg, etc., or Marvel's *Avengers*, which includes Spider-Man, Iron Man, Thor, Hulk, Captain America, Ant Man, and others.

Some people may think the reason companies do this is to draw in the fan bases of multiple characters to generate a bigger viewership. That's definitely part of it. But the real value of inhabiting these shared universes is that they improve the probability of success with subsequent projects because they are part of a collection of interconnected, scalable IP. Valiant had implemented this strategy originally, but under Acclaim's ownership they had discontinued it. We brought it back in full force.

With this understanding in place, the question remained whether we should just focus on film and television deals and forget publishing altogether. What we learned was that while traditional publishing may be a low-margin, high-cost endeavour, it was important to keep the fanboy comic book world excited with new content. That was particularly true for Valiant, because our universe of 1,500 characters had been out of view for years when we bought the company. So we needed to make the storylines fresh and current. Even if a comic book sold, say, 100,000 copies, great reviews and online excitement on fan forums would be useful when pitching movie studios on why a character from the nineties was still relevant to today's audiences. It was also great low-cost creative research and development tool that signalled which characters and stories resonated for other media.

The same went for consumer products, like T-shirts, character figurines, or toys. Even though these sort of deals only generated modest revenue, they went a long way in helping raise brand awareness and generating a buzz. Because we remained a relatively small outfit—roughly twenty full-time employees and about 200 freelancers at our peak—we never had a massive advertising budget. But if we did a product deal for a Valiant t-shirt, consumers would become walking billboards advertising our brand and characters. That, in turn, helped build brand equity.

What we were learning was that the word—*equity*—was about much more than landing one or two big random deals. It was about creating an ecosystem of interconnected, cross-pollinated value propositions that, together, could generate serious, sustainable value. Gaining that deep understanding proved to be the epiphany that parted the dark corporate clouds and shone a column of radiant light to illumine our way forward.

When people are passionate about what you are doing and see that you have an exciting mission and viable strategy, assembling partners, investors, and employees gets much easier. With the IP secured, and the optimal strategy and business plan firmly in place, attracting serious talent was not the uphill climb it had been previously.

We attracted top talent to the management team like Marvel's former award-winning editor Warren Simmons, the former president and COO of Wizard Fred Pierce, and former head of consumer products and promotions at Marvel Russ Brown—a leader who had been at Marvel during the early stages of building their consumer products business that went on to become one of the top 10 largest in the world.

You may be wondering how a twenty-something CEO like me was able to lead a management team whose age and experience exceeded mine. I made my share of mistakes along the way and learned through trial and error. Initially I erred by being more authoritative than collaborative. Then I realized my error and changed. My improved approach was to learn through experience, utilize soft skills to effectively manage more senior team members, and use responsibility and compensation as tools to help demonstrate respect and recognition.

As a young entrepreneur, many of the people you hire are going to be older than you. You need to acquire the skills to manage and respect them while still maintaining control of what's in the best interests of your business. Doing so will make you a better asset and will bring a wealth of knowledge and expertise to your business in the form of experienced talent.

With key management hires in place, we also added major heavyweights to our senior advisory board, such as: former Marvel Chief Financial Officer (CFO) Ken West, former Marvel Chief Operating Officer (COO) and President Bill Jemas, Pixar's former Chief Marketing Officer (CMO) Donald Evans, former

Electronic Arts worldwide studio chief Bruce McMillan, and legendary entertainment attorney Peter Dekom, who was named by *Premier* magazine as one of the fifty most powerful people in Hollywood.

~

To have assembled such talent was humbling and inspiring. Hiring high-calibre individuals who have already accomplished what you are setting out to do—especially from a similar stage in a company's lifecycle—dramatically increases an entrepreneur's odds of success. We now had a brain trust to provide wise counsel as the rounds of investor funding increased, the deals got bigger, and the stakes grew higher.

Of course, like any entrepreneurial venture, all along we had constantly been reaching out to investors to generate cash. We pitched over 100 investors and got turned down by all of them. All. Of. Them!

For most traditional investors, Valiant Entertainment didn't make much sense. We were not an established operating business. Moreover, we were not a tech start-up. That meant we had to turn to non-traditional investors. Here's how desperate I was: I actually hit up a martial arts teacher for an investment. During our meeting he got so bored that he fell asleep in front of me. Total humiliation. I would rather have taken a roundhouse kick to the ribs!

In the end, I later decided to focus on investors who already possessed a deep understanding of the entertainment business. Specifically, I honed in on former Marvel investors and larger investors. Eventually, that's where we raised the money. An investment deal with a higher valuation did emerge, but we chose to go with a lower valuation because we wanted to choose the right partner by having a former Marvel CEO on our side, which I believed was key. But the point is that when it comes to raising investments, you cannot quit in the face of rejection.

Like I said from the start, entrepreneurship is not for everyone. Over 100 investors told me no. But I knew what we had was valuable and worthy of investment. If you believe the same about your product or company, you must press forward with confidence and resilience.

Over our lifecycle we went through several rounds of funding, including support from investors like former Marvel CEO Peter Cuneo, early investors in Legendary Pictures (the company known for producing hits like Christopher Nolan's *The Dark Knight* trilogy and *300*), and Chinese media group DMG Entertainment, which co-produced Marvel's *Iron Man 3* and helped the movie break box-office records in China.

Having cracked the code on the right business model and strategy for creating value, I now understood how to communicate to industry insiders with clarity and confidence. Or, to put it another way, having put in the hours doing deep research, I now knew what the hell I was talking about—and it showed.

Beyond fundraising, another core part of building our business involved securing print and digital publishing distribution deals. And in that regard, Valiant did some of the best deals in the industry. The trick? We didn't accept standard deals and got creative and tough with our negotiations. Doing so significantly increased our reach and placement in retails stores and online. This was crucial, because it allowed us to aggressively build our brand in the market.

In parallel, we also built direct relationships with all the major retailers. We worked hard to treat them as partners. This helped us gain strong supporters for our products and drive sales even higher. To maximize this effort, I hired a former 'top 10' retailer with strong domain expertise and existing relationships. Moreover, we invested heavily in our initial content and began the work with significant lead time to ensure our content quality wasn't compromised.

We knew we would have less time and money for subsequent series but wanted to ensure we started with a bang and built a strong initial sales track record that would set an important precedent. Warren and Fred did a good job, and I tried to provide sufficient time and resources to flourish.

Another important part of building the business involved locking up premium consumer product deals with blue-chip mid-tier licensees. We had to take a realistic approach. Large licensees were only interested in the brands that already had mass appeal, such as Star Wars. The mid-tier segment, however, held opportunities if we were patient and were willing to compromise on economics to get the best partners. We quickly realized there was a snowball effect, as landing each new blue-chip partner helped us get the next one as our credibility grew.

To expand the brand equity beyond the direct terms of each deal, we also made sure there was a significant promotional and marketing spend requirement in every deal we did. Russ proved critical in calling in a lot of favours to push deals across the finish line—one more advantage of having a veteran with a large Rolodex who had made mountains of money for Marvel licensees.

And of course, one of the most crucial aspects of building the Valiant business came in the form of the major motion picture contracts I negotiated on some of our most popular characters. Initially, we were in talks with Paramount about my childhood favourite, Harbinger. When they low-balled us, I pushed back. Their response was basically that I was new in town and that I was lucky to even be talking to them, so I should be quiet and grateful. It was a classic example of movie industry 'big leaguing'—trying to muscle the little guy into obedience to win the deal at the lowest price. So I did what I thought was best. I pulled out.

I'm glad I did. I realized that part of the problem was that I was taking old characters to Hollywood and getting disappointing results. So, I changed strategy, re-launched characters successfully in the aforementioned publishing deals, and revitalized them into hot 'new' characters. With a fresh coat of 'paint' on the characters, we then partnered with leading producers, funded and developed screenplays crafted by top writers, and then re-pitched the projects to studios.

By partnering with leading producers, we were able to leverage their experience and relationships to lock down larger deals with the biggest movie studios. We also funded the screenplays so we would have more control over the creative process and provide more value to the studios.

Eventually, we raised and allocated capital from DMG Entertainment to co-finance the production of film projects. This made us one of the few parties outside of major studios with this capability. We partnered with producers like Original Film (*Fast and the Furious* franchise), Sean Daniel (*The Mummy* franchise) and the Russo Brothers (*Avengers* franchise), writers like J. Michael Straczynski (*Thor*) and Oscar-winner Eric Heisserer (*Arrival*), as well as directors like Brett Ratner (*Rush Hour* franchise) and Matthew Vaughn (*X-Men: First Class*).

Dinesh and I were an effective tandem—bringing together the creative and business sides respectively. Now, with the hard work of our business building strategy in motion, we re-entered Hollywood from this renewed position of strength and negotiated a five-movie deal with Sony for *Bloodshot*, *Harbinger*, the *Bloodshot* sequel, the *Harbinger* sequel, and then Bloodshot and Harbinger coming together in a final film. Those Valiant deals represent the collective efforts of our entire team, including our sagacious advisory board.

Indeed, seldom are a company's victories the work of a single person. As a young entrepreneur, it is vital that you try to surround yourself with people who have domain and functional expertise—people who have done it well before in their specialized areas of responsibility. By doing this you will reduce execution risk and boost fundraising from seasoned investors who see an experienced team.

In the case of landing major movie deals, Peter Dekom's mentorship was vital. To date, the five movie deals we did with Sony Pictures each remain some of the most lucrative film and merchandising deals ever done for a similar intellectual property, and are nearly identical to the deal Marvel did with Sony on *Spider-Man*.

Another key input was Bill Jemas's counsel and insight, which proved crucial in successfully re-launching IP in publishing to build our consumer products. I'll never forget the first time Bill Jemas invited me to be his guest for the Marvel screening of *Iron Man*, the first movie they made marking the creation of Marvel Studios. Prior to this, all Marvel movies had been made by major Hollywood studios (*X-Men* by Fox, *Hulk* by Universal, *Spider-Man* by Sony).

This was a big moment for Marvel, one filled with a lot of uncertainty about whether using a former drug addict and scandal-ridden actor like Robert Downey Jr as their lead character would pay off. Likewise, Director Jon Favreau had never made a movie of this scale and was known more as an actor. Even the *Iron Man* trailer was getting mixed reviews. Everything was on the line.

Bill and I entered the venue. There stood Stan Lee. I glanced around the venue. A few paces away were famous *Iron Man* comic creators Bob Layton (who also played a key role at Valiant) and Marvel CCO Joe Quesada, who had also been with Valiant during the early days. We all sat down for the screening. Bill and I sat behind the *Iron Man* creators. I paid careful attention to their reactions. It was clear they were seeing the film for the first time. At moments, tears welled up in their eyes. Their lifelong work and dreams were now made manifest on the big screen. I felt excited for them. The movie was, of course, a dazzling mix of science fiction, action, adventure, and comedy.

Downey, Favreau, and Marvel had created a legacy blockbuster. When the final scene rolled, everyone in the screening room shot up from their seats in a standing ovation. That moment—frozen in my memory—wasn't just a game-changer for comic history, but entertainment history as well. A few years later, they sold the company to Disney for $4.5 billion.

Marvel continued making its own movies after *Iron Man* and created the biggest string of hits in Hollywood history, including most recently *Avengers: Endgame,* which smashed box office records. I couldn't thank Bill enough for bringing me to the event to be there to witness movie history in the making. He has always been a gracious friend and to this day insists I call him my 'Uncle Bill'. Bottom line: great mentors make a world of difference. They did for me and Valiant.

Our company was now on a roll. Valiant soon had the highest selling characters behind Marvel and DC, was named Publisher of the Year, and was eventually nominated for over ninety awards. We raised a total of $140 million—$40 million for business growth and $100 million into a separate company (independently owned by investors) to exclusively co-finance Valiant movies—our very own mini-version of Marvel Studios. It was one of the largest fundraises ever done for a superhero entertainment company.

To finally be building a serious entertainment company felt professionally rewarding. As an equity holder, I was encouraged by the deals we were doing. And as CEO, I was elated by the quality of work Dinesh and the creative team were generating.

The business that had floundered for two years while immersed in a trademark war—and that family and friends said we should abandon—was finally gaining market share and was already worth many, many times what we'd bought it for in bankruptcy.

Things were finally looking up. About the only thing missing in my life at the time was ... a girl.

6

Life and Business Aren't Linear

STROLLING THROUGH NEW York City at night can make even the most unsentimental cynic feel a rush of whimsy and romance. After finishing up my daily work for Valiant, I'd often sling on a coat and take in the cool evening air with a brisk walk through the Big Apple. The city was a blur of faces, lights, motion, and colour.

The serenity of Central Park in fall, the electrifying spectacle of Times Square at midnight, the fashionable energy of Fifth Avenue, the bustling theatre lines on Broadway—there's a reason New York is known as 'the city that never sleeps'. Passing by smiling couples holding hands on the sidewalk made me long for companionship, someone to share life's simple pleasures with. To be young and in love in New York City looked magical. Little did I know, my family had been conspiring to ensure I experienced it all firsthand.

In case you don't already know, let's establish one thing right away. If there is one certitude in life—one transcendent truth that spans all space and time—it is this: no one, and I mean *no one*, can play matchmaker like an Indian family. If you are young, Indian, and single, I assure you that right now Mom, Dad, Auntie, or Uncle are surveying the dating landscape and hunting to find you a suitable future spouse. There is something endearing (if somewhat intrusive and suffocating) about our elders' unrivalled cultural dominance in the matchmaking arena. They love big, and they want to see us carry on the rich tradition of forming and maintaining strong families. So when my Uncle Anil called from Cherry Hill, New Jersey, to tell me about a wonderful girl in nearby Pennsylvania, all I could do was smile and agree to call her.

The idea of courtship had its allure. But at the time, I wasn't sure how much I had to offer a prospective dating partner. While things with Valiant had stabilized from the early days, it was still the inevitable entrepreneurial roller coaster where I was working long CEO hours and making relatively little money. If I was going to dip my toe back into the dating world I wanted to be able to do so with an open heart and give it my all. My uncle had possessed the wisdom to take me to Atlantic City to buy that rare Valiant comic book when I was a teenager. *Who knows,* I thought, *maybe Uncle has an incredible girl for me.*

'She's very special', Uncle told me. 'Her name is Anaya. She's an Indian-American from a wonderful family. She's smart, educated, beautiful, and has great values.' After previous dating experiences, that last part—strong values—appealed to me. 'Jason, just promise me you'll call her and keep an open mind,' he pleaded. I gave Uncle my word that I would call her.

Anaya answered the phone with a warm and welcoming demeanour. We chuckled about how our families had conspired to introduce us. She was intelligent, funny, and a great listener. Towards the end of our call I said we should grab dinner the next time she was in the city. A couple weeks later, we set a date.

When we met in person, our connection was immediate. The usual first-date awkwardness dissipated quickly; within minutes we were laughing and carrying on like old friends. Uncle hadn't embellished about her looks either; she was striking.

Anaya said she was in medical school studying to be a doctor. 'My passion is helping people in their greatest time of need,' she said. Money and status weren't what motivated her, 'Family is the most important thing in life', she explained. I liked that.

We also bonded over our mutually shared heritage. 'You're Gujarati?' she asked excitedly. 'No way! I am, too!' I found her stories about growing up Indian in America fascinating. She was much more westernized and liberal than I was. But she liked my strong streak of Indian pride and humoured me by listening intently to stories of my beloved Rajkot. Most of all, she seemed to take genuine interest in my life. Anaya said she thought my entrepreneurial journey was exciting, honourable even, as I had followed my childhood dreams. By the end of our first date I was, in a word, captivated.

The day after our first date my parents just *happened* to call me. And, by some random and unplanned coincidence, they just *happened* to ask about my dating life. I had to chuckle.

'Well,' I said, 'I'm sure Uncle told you all about Anaya. Let's just say he did a great job fixing me up.' Mom was encouraged at the prospect of me dating a well-educated Indian girl from a great family. 'It was just one date, Mom,' I cautioned. 'But she's lovely. I'm definitely interested.'

In the months ahead, Anaya and I spent as much as time as we could together. Between my running Valiant and Anaya's medical school studies in Pennsylvania, coordinating schedules was tricky. Nevertheless, we agreed our relationship was worth the effort. Like all couples, we had our ups and downs. Perhaps because we were brought up in different cultures, differences in thinking and lifestyles became more apparent. But we came to appreciate each other's peculiarities.

After about a year of dating one another, the inevitable discussions about marriage arose. Every few weeks Anaya would pepper our conversations with not-so-subtle hints. 'I'm waiting for you to propose to me,' she'd say with a nervous smile. 'I really want to marry you.'

My heart was tugging me in that direction, but my head wasn't there yet. Valiant was doing quite well by this point. But since our goal was to keep salaries to a reasonable level and leave as much equity in the company as possible, I was not in a strong financial position personally. There was also the issue of our parents' approval. When the subject came up during family conversations, my dad reminded me that I might not be ready to be a husband yet.

'Your grandfather has gotten to know Anaya's parents,' my father said. "They are truly wonderful people. But I feel there's something I must say, my son. You're not earning the kind of money necessary to support a family,' he said. 'Do you think you're really ready to get married? You're very busy with Valiant, and things are really taking off now.'

'Well, Dad, a person doesn't have to be a millionaire to get married,' I said. 'I see a lot of people getting married who don't have much money. And you know what? They're happy. Things seem to work out just fine.'

'Yes, but being a husband and father means you're responsible for others,' he said. 'It's not like living the bachelor lifestyle you're accustomed to. You have to think beyond yourself. Your wife and children must come first in all things. Anaya is also five years younger than you. She has more schooling ahead of her. Supporting her goal of being a doctor is very important.'

He had a point. Several, actually. I definitely respected his wisdom. He was coming from a pure place of care and concern. He was a very supportive husband to my mother's educational and professional aspirations. That was one of the many things I always admired about him. Anaya's mother, like mine, had an impressive educational pedigree. She was also a doctor. Anaya said she wanted to follow in her mother's medical footsteps. I didn't want to do anything to disrupt her path or impede her dream. Despite the seeds of doubt, however, my mind found ways to whisk them away.

Plenty of married couples make it through medical school together, I told myself. *Besides, I love her and she loves me. She's special. Yes, we have some differences. But those are relatively small compared to the feelings we have for one another. Many people spend a lifetime searching and never find love. You know what? I'm going to go ahead with this. I am going to propose to Anaya.*

The following week I began visiting jewellery stores. I knew her preferences and went in search of the perfect engagement ring. After I picked out a ring, I waited to buy it until I paid Anaya's father a visit in person to ask his permission to marry his daughter. I planned to go in a couple days.

In the interim, Anaya mentioned she was feeling a bit strange. 'I'm feeling a little off,' she said. 'It's likely nothing. But I think I'm gonna go get a check-up just to be safe.' Her tone was so casual I thought little of it. 'Yeah, that sounds like a good idea,' I said. 'You're probably right. I'm sure it's fine.'

The next day I summoned the courage to visit Anaya's father.

'Uncle, I want to propose to Anaya,' I told him. 'We truly love each other. I believe we will have a beautiful life together. I promise to take care of her and love her like she deserves to be loved.' To my relief, he was overjoyed. 'You have my full and complete blessing,' he said. 'We are so happy about this news!' The euphoric reception reconfirmed my belief that proposing to her was the right decision. That night I was swept up in the rapturous winds of romance. Everything felt right in the world.

And then, the very next day, our world began spinning off its axis.

Anaya's doctors scanned her body. When the results came back, given her medical background, she didn't need anyone to explain how catastrophic they were. She called me immediately.

'I'm at work,' she said. 'I really need to see you.'

'Okay. What's wrong?'

'I just need to see you.'

'What's going on?'

'The scan. It's bad. Like, really bad.'

'Wait, what do you mean?'

She began to cry.

'So you have to take some medicine or something?' I asked nervously. 'We'll get through it.'

'No' she said sobbing. 'Jason, I have ... cancer.'

'What? What are you talking about? There must be some mistake,' I said.

'I read the scan myself,' she said. 'It's there. It's cancer.'

'Okay ... ok ... I'm coming to you. I love you. We will get you through this. I'll be right there.'

No one is ever prepared for that moment. The power of the 'C-word'—cancer—is uniquely devastating. On my way to comfort Anaya, I rehearsed in my mind ways to lift her spirits and soften the blow. *Maybe it's one of those early-stage situations*, I said in my mind, like an actor preparing for a performance. *They call it 'cancer', but they're able to kill it quick.* Then another: *This was just one test. We need to get more tests with different doctors to get a second and third opinion.*

When I arrived, we met at her family's home.

'I can't tell my parents,' she said sobbing.

'Why?' I asked.

'I just don't know how to say it to them,' she said as I held her. 'Can you tell them for me?'

'You want *me* to tell them?'

'Yes.'

We sat her mother and father down.

'Uncle, Auntie, there's some really bad news,' I said. 'Anaya went to the doctor and had some tests. The results indicate that she has cancer.'

Their shock and disbelief were instant.

Since her mother was a doctor, she agreed we needed to have more tests conducted by more cancer specialists. And that's exactly what we did. But each test confirmed the cancer diagnosis—only worse.

'It's definitely late-stage breast cancer,' a doctor told me when Anaya wasn't in the room. 'Based on the scans, it's not clear how far the cancer has penetrated. It appears to be very borderline, as to whether it has invaded the chest wall or not.'

'What does that mean?', I asked.

'Well, if the cancer has gone that deep and metastasized, the solutions available become extremely limited.'

'I don't understand,' I said frantically. 'There's no solution?'

'Well … at that stage there would be very little we could do,' he said. 'We just don't know yet.'

'But … how is this possible? She's only twenty-six. How … I mean … I just don't understand.'

I felt dizzy, like I'd tumbled into another dimension.

Anaya began getting treatments in Philadelphia. Later, using some business relationships I'd made through Valiant, I was able to get her transferred to Memorial Sloan Kettering Cancer Center in New York, one of the best cancer-treatment institutes in the world. Fortunately, her health insurance covered the enormous treatment cost. To make the process easier, she stayed with me so I could take care of her.

Early on she made the decision to take the more Western approach and pursue the traditional path of chemotherapy, radiation, and aggressive surgery. She understood the medical realities and risks. I supported her personal decision, of course. But unlike her, I was not educated on the physical and psychological effects such treatments can produce.

I researched what I could online. I wanted to be as knowledgeable as possible. The more I studied, the more barbaric and inhumane it all seemed. The treatments were taking an enormous toll on her body, mind, and spirit. How could they not? The sickness, vomiting, permanent cutting out of her breasts, inability to have children, loss of her hair, loss of her fingernails, loss of weight, the weakness, the frailty—it was brutal. I felt helpless watching her wither and being unable to stop it. Yet her courage and bravery throughout reconfirmed all the reasons I'd fallen in love with her in the first place.

There are so many frozen moments in my mind from that time period. Most involve the extreme juxtaposition of brutality and beauty. Like sweeping up the clumps of her hair that had fallen onto the floor of my apartment, and tearing up when placing them in the wastebasket. Or helping her get to the bathroom during the night to vomit and catching a glimpse of her face while wondering how it was possible to be that sick and pretty at the same time. Indeed, amid the ravages of her battle against cancer, her heart and will to fight were arresting in their beauty.

My spirituality sustained me during this period. Turning to faith during a time of struggle and adversity may seem clichéd. But it's commonplace for a reason: it brings great solace and support. I started re-reading my books on Jain and Buddhist philosophy and beliefs. I'd also located a large Jain temple just two hours north of the city. I'd never been to a temple like that before. The first time I visited I was unfamiliar with all the rules. When I put money in the donation box, I was unaware I was supposed to walk backwards, away from it without turning around. Later, when speaking with a temple leader, I apologized for my ignorance about the proper protocols.

'Don't you worry,' he said with a big smile. 'It's no problem at all. When I went to temple for the first time, I didn't know either! What matters most is a person's intentions and heart, not the rules they follow.' I appreciated his words of kindness. His counsel also encouraged me to worry less whether I was praying 'the right way' and instead focus on praying with the right spirit.

After months of gut-wrenching treatments, the doctors finally declared that Anaya was effectively in a holding pattern. They had done all they could do, had completed the full cycle of treatments and surgery, and she had stabilized. All that was left to do was maintain and monitor her health and let her get back to her school and work routines. Yet while the physical effects had temporarily ceased taking their toll, the emotional and mental upheaval had not.

One day after work I came home and Anaya wasn't there. I called her phone but she didn't answer. I panicked. For two hours I dialled and got nothing. Then she stumbled through the door of my apartment. She had gone to a nearby bar and drowned her pain in alcohol. It was the sort of action I could relate to from the wilder days of my youth. It was also the first of many behaviours that began to manifest as the psychological fallout caught up to the physical trauma she'd endured.

Then several weeks later, when I returned from Los Angeles on a business trip, she informed me that she had developed feelings for someone else and was going to move on. I couldn't believe what I heard. Despite multiple attempts, she remained steadfast in her decision. Suddenly, we were finished.

The soul-crushing sense of devastation I experienced back then feels much different today. Initially, I blamed myself; perhaps I took out some of my entrepreneurial stress on her. Yet with the passage of time, I gained greater clarity. Later on I realized that what seemed like erratic behaviour on her part was likely her subconscious way of severing the negative association of me with her cancer battle.

In fact, several months after our relationship was over she reached out to say she was sorry, that she wasn't in her right state of mind, and that she couldn't believe the choices she had made. I appreciated her call, but she didn't need to apologize or explain. If Jainism had taught me anything it was that: 'Karma is the root cause of birth and death, and these are said to be the source of misery. None can escape the effect of their own past karma.'

I'd meditated on all that transpired. Doing that interior work helped reclaim inner peace. I realized that it didn't matter whether I could understand it or not, I accepted that this was part of my karma and destiny. As an entrepreneur, I'd conditioned myself to believe that business stretches people past their natural limits. But being in love with someone confronting a fatal illness brings the fragility of life into focus like few things can.

It made me realize that life can change in a nanosecond; that relationships are as delicate as eggshells; and that we gain a panoramic perspective of what matters most in life when our tolerance for emotional pain and discomfort get bent to the breaking point.

I already believed the age-old truth that what doesn't kill you, makes you stronger. My time in Thailand at the Muay Tai fighting camp had taught me how to absorb extreme physical pain. But watching my partner face mortality only to lose her to someone else pushed my tolerance for emotional pain to a new level of strength.

The experience taught me something else. So many of the things we perceive in business as 'big' and 'dire' aren't. Today, sometimes I catch myself telling a colleague, 'Come on … this isn't life or death. Relax already!' That's also when I'm reminded that life and business are not linear. You can spend your whole life mapping out pristine personal and professional plans only to watch them get torn to shreds as unforeseen forces impinge on you from all sides.

Don't count on your life's events unfolding in a predictable pattern. About the only thing that is certain is that nothing is certain.

Walking the cancer journey alongside the person I planned to marry also taught me to live in the moment. Be present. Show appreciation. And be grateful for all things. I think most people know these things intellectually. But it's another thing to live and absorb these lessons firsthand.

Some people try to trick themselves into thinking they can compartmentalize life from business. Such segregation is neither possible nor preferable. Instead of viewing life and work as separate spheres, I prefer to see them as one. Like water changing from liquid to ice, work and life are comprised of the same essence: you. This means the goal of any great leader isn't to avoid difficult experiences; rather, to absorb them, learn from them, and allow the lessons to flow back into the stream of life and business to propel you farther along your journey. For me, putting this belief into practise meant not just letting go of a relationship I loved, but a business as well.

My decision to exit Valiant and eventually sell my ownership stake was a difficult one. From 2007 to 2013, I had served as CEO and seen our small team of twenty or so full-time staff and approximately hundred freelancers work together to grow a bankrupt comic book company into a $100,000,000 entertainment powerhouse with a stellar reputation, generating a record return in the industry. For example, *The New York Times* had hailed us as the next Marvel, and the *Economic Times* magazine had written a glowing cover story on us.

I was humbled to have been given the chance to work alongside talented and devoted colleagues who gave their all. Ironically, though, the better Valiant did, the rockier my relationship with Dinesh became.

When recognition and money are on the line, people's character, similarities, and differences become more evident. Choosing the right partner in business involves ensuring that you share the same vision and common values. Often, the people you end up going into business with are old friends, who are close to you due to the circumstances at that time, such as a college roommate or neighbour. But in many cases, business partnerships forged out of convenience or proximity lack the proper alignment of vision and values necessary to make an enduring business partnership. Moreover, people change. Sometimes the right business partner today will not be the right business partner tomorrow as their or your vision and values shift or evolve.

As for the business side of my decision to exit Valiant, there were many variables that collectively let me know it was time to go. For one, our valuation had capped out; the only thing that could drive it higher would be movies, which were largely out of our control and dependent on third-party film studios. We felt it would take a minimum of five years (an optimistic view) to actually release the first movie. Even then, as is customary in the movie industry, Valiant would only have consultation rights on films with zero control on timing or content.

Second, I knew that leaving as the CEO was an opportunity to monetize my stake in the company, as otherwise investors want you to keep the majority of your stake as skin in the game and motivation. Phasing out my tenure from a company that began with college-dreams built on my childhood heroes was emotional. Valiant was our baby. We'd turned one person's trash into our very own treasure. Still, I knew in my heart it was time for me to move on to explore new challenges and opportunities.

One of the biggest questions entrepreneurs ask me is: how do I know when it's the right time to exit? It's an important and vexing issue all entrepreneurs eventually confront. Complicating matters is the fact that you can get so attached to what you've created that it blurs your ability to see things objectively. Like an artist who brushes their vision onto a canvas, entrepreneurs translate the vision in their minds into a physical creation called a company. So how does one separate their emotional attachments to a business in order to make a smart, rational decision on when to leave? While every situation is unique, let me give you a few pieces of advice.

First, if you have an opportunity to change your life by exiting, take the money, at least in a partial exit. Second, once you change your life financially, do not bet it all again and again, especially when the business is not in your control. Third, understand that you are unlikely to grow and evolve as an entrepreneur or leader without a diverse set of experiences, including with respect to geography, industry, company size, stage, market context, and culture. Why? Because wide-ranging experiences hone your ability to confront a critical mass of data points and see patterns and opportunities. And finally, when considering an exit, you also need to assess not just the financial terms but also whether the company's future trajectory still aligns with your vision and values.

In the case of Valiant, I knew that the next phase of growth was dependent on the decisions of third-party movie studios. That meant it was no longer a true entrepreneurial opportunity with complete control; rather, it had morphed into more of an investor/speculator game. With the movie studios now serving as a sort of gatekeeper to growth, the business model moving forward was not strong or ideal. Bottom line: as hard as it was for me, I knew it was time to begin letting go of Valiant.

I knew we'd placed Valiant Entertainment on firm ground with a bright future ahead. As CEO, I'd done the deal to buy the assets, fixed the legal problems, hired each of our incredible team members, even leased the office and bought the furniture, developed and implemented the strategy, did the deals with our investors, led our board meetings, and brokered our deals. So I felt like I was leaving my family. Our team had battled against impossible odds, persevered, and won. As I mentioned though, some personal relationships, like mine and Dinesh's, had become strained under the pressure of battling for so many years.

I offered to serve in the capacity of vice chairman, a position I held from 2013 to 2015. Dinesh took over as CEO and continued as CCO. I sold my stake to one of our core investors, DMG, in tranches that concluded in 2017. The following year, Dinesh sold his stake to DMG and officially exited Valiant as well. People often ask me how I will feel when Valiant's blockbuster films, like *Bloodshot*—written by Oscar-nominated Eric Heisserer, featuring actor Vin Diesel—are released in movie theatres across the globe. Will I lament having left? Or regret exiting the biggest superhero entertainment company behind Marvel and DC Comics? My answer is always the same. I will feel a deep sense of pride. Having the chance to complete that film deal, and others like it during my tenure as Valiant's CEO, afforded me the chance to help cement the company's legacy as an enduring global brand.

When films like *Bloodshot*, *Harbinger*, or *Shadowman* launch worldwide, I'll be like the millions of fans eagerly lining up at the box office to watch our childhood heroes splash across the big screen!

Valiant will always hold a special place in my heart. It was my first entrepreneurial success. Moreover, it was an idea built from the dreams of my youth. During all those years holed up in my childhood bedroom, with my eyes glued to my coveted Valiant comic books, those characters had stoked my imagination and fuelled my creativity. To have been given the chance to rescue them from the dustbin of history and leave them in strong hands felt richly rewarding.

Valiant produced another benefit, one I found personally liberating. The success of my Valiant deal afforded me the freedom to never have to accept a position that didn't excite me. I still remember the rush of freedom that fell over me when the money finally hit the bank account. I picked up the phone and dialled my mom and dad.

'I have something important to tell you,' I said with an emotional lilt in my voice. 'This family will not need to worry about money.' It was a milestone moment in my relationship with my parents. I was redeemed. A wave of peacefulness washed over my relationship with my parents—one that completely changed our dynamic for the better.

To be able to give my parents security and peace of mind forever ... well, there are no words to describe it.

Despite having hit a turning point professionally and personally, as a purebred entrepreneur, I knew I couldn't remain on the sidelines for long. There's always another deal, another challenge, another opportunity to assemble an all-star team to tackle massive problems and create value. The fun and fulfilment you derive from it all is addictive. No longer having to make career decisions based on a paycheck, but on my passion—*that* was the real achievement. My exit helped me grow as a person and a business leader. In the wake of Valiant's success, several large funds wanted to back me to do another acquisition and turnaround.

'Entrepreneurship by acquisition' was a concept I was willing to explore. Atari, the first and most iconic gaming company—the place where Steve Jobs got his start—was bankrupt. Snapping it up would bring with it IP in the form of classic games. The strategy would be to reinvent games for modern audiences through a 360-degree IP exploitation across film, TV, print, digital, and consumer products.

Then a former Atari executive took over the company's debt and took control of the creditors committee, before setting a high minimum bid requirement that no one would meet. He then converted the debt to equity and took over the company. Even though investors were willing to back me and bid over the minimum bid, I didn't think that move was justifiable, nor would it bring the investors a strong result. Better to be fair, honest, and keep eyes peeled for opportunities.

For a time, I thought that one of those opportunities might come in the form of Archie Comics. Two different families had 50:50 control over Archie Comics that frequently resulted in a deadlock over the business's direction. The company owned and controlled the IP for the entire Archie universe of characters across all forms of media. The brand's roster of classic characters made it an enticing property that had attracted interested investors for years. Over the course of a year I'd spent time with one of the two families to gain a deeper understanding of their vision for the brand and to gain trust should they ever decide to sell their controlling stake.

Eventually, the family offered me access to an exclusive deal to take a controlling stake in the company, along with the family's board seat. But, after meeting with the other family who controlled the remaining 50 per cent of the company, I realized they wanted to maintain control; gaining operating control would require me to engage in a hostile board takeover.

I'd rather miss an opportunity than wrest control of a company away from its founder's family. I was grateful to have built a strong relationship with the initial family, and was thankful for their offer to give me access to an exclusive deal. But as a co-owner of Valiant myself, I had a deep and abiding appreciation for the bonds founders and owners have with their businesses. There was no way I was getting sucked into forcibly breaking up a family's company. So, I passed.

Finally, for a time a potential proposed sale of ACK Media piqued my interest. During my time in Rajkot and Mumbai I'd become familiar and fond of Amar Chitra Katha comics. So when I saw a news article that founder and chairman of Future Group, Kishore Biyani, the majority and controlling shareholder, and another key shareholder, Gaurav Burman (director of Dabur International) were considering selling ACK, I took notice.

What if I could launch an ACK 2.0 strategy similar to the Valiant 2.0 plan and revamp its content for modern audiences?

ACK's character universe is rooted in Indian spirituality, mythology, and history—also offering a chance to create a positive cultural impact.

However, at the final stage of what was a six-month process, Kishore backed out. As it turned out, he had a deep emotional connection with the business and couldn't let go of its control. Nevertheless, I enjoyed my interactions with him, found him to be a very dynamic and passionate entrepreneur and this also gave me the opportunity to reconnect with Mumbai.

Atari, Archie Comics, and ACK Media weren't meant to be. Still, when I surveyed the business world around me, I saw opportunities on all sides. I knew that when I found something I was passionate about, I would be all in. And if that were the case, I might as well live and work where I felt most at home, the place where I belonged. So, after several months of travelling, I made a very informed decision to leave New York City and come home.

I resolved that wherever the work happens, it happens. Deals and opportunities come and go. The first priority in my personal life was to settle in the land I love most, the one I didn't get to grow up in as a child.

I packed my bags, waved the Big Apple goodbye, hopped on a jet headed for Mumbai, and never looked back.

7

Push Yourself Harder than You Do Others

NO SOONER HAD the jet wheels kissed the runway in Mumbai that my stomach started grumbling. The sixteen-hour flight was exhausting, but nothing was going to keep me from feasting on my favourite foods. I hopped in a taxi and told the driver to take me straight to Matunga. Along the ride, I rolled down the windows to soak in the sights. The honking cars, the swerving in and out of lanes, the balmy Mumbai breeze against my face—I felt alive. Home.

I struggled to decide which of my two favourite restaurants—Anand Bhavan or Idli House—to go to first before settling on the former. The driver pulled up. I darted for the door. *Uttappam, rava dosa, masala dosa, dahi vada, sheera, gulab jamun*—I felt like ordering one of everything on the menu. (Friends tease me that I do business like a Gujarati but spend money like a Punjabi). Such a simple pleasure, eating. Especially at Anand Bhavan. Delicious food, great value, and a super friendly staff. (Visit on any given Sunday and you're likely to see me grabbing lunch.) To hell with jet lag, there was no way I wasn't getting my food fix before crashing in a bed!

My first couple weeks back in India were spent reconnecting with family and friends. People had gotten married, had children, bought homes, and grown their families. I felt grateful to be back in their lives and have them back in mine. Sharing, laughing, rejuvenating, reminiscing—those first few weeks in Mumbai were a welcome sabbatical from business. When people asked about my next endeavours, I told them the truth: I had no idea, no plan. I was in no hurry to rush into my next innings. Having served as Valiant CEO, I had enjoyed the responsibilities that come with executive leadership and entrepreneurship. Whatever my next move, I wanted to force myself to stretch my skills and tackle larger challenges than those I'd already encountered. When the right opportunity presented itself, I would feel that fire in the belly.

Before long, India's tight-knit investor and venture capital communities began reaching out after they heard I was in town. Soon, a series of informal meetings were set up to get acquainted. I viewed the sessions as a chance to learn more about the market, expand my network, and forge new relationships. Ironically, the less I seemed to project an interest in landing new career opportunities, the more flowed my way.

I've found that sometimes the less aggressive you are in selling and promoting yourself, the more people seek you out. Come off as desperate and you kill deals and opportunities. Likewise, if you give off an air of cockiness or arrogance, you'll repel prospects. A confident, humble self-presentation hits the sweet spot.

You have at least two core assets as an entrepreneur: capital and your own abilities. Valiant had given me the former; I wanted to focus on sharpening the latter. I was entering a new phase of my life and entrepreneurial journey. The days of youthful foolishness had faded long ago. Now I wanted to mature and scale my abilities by leading larger teams, overcoming greater business obstacles. I remained patient in seeking opportunities to expand my CEO leadership skills.

Initially, I was approached about coming on as the CEO of a large food-delivery company. They were on the edge of receiving an infusion of $50 million in funding. The founder was bright and enthusiastic. He said their goal was to go from eight cities to twenty. I was grateful for the offer. But the expansion plan didn't light my world on fire. Besides, the business was seemingly on auto-pilot. Where was the fun in that?

'You can find a lot of other people who can keep a steady hand on the wheel,' I told him. 'I appreciate you thinking of me. I truly do. I just don't think that's really gonna get me out of bed every day. I've got to be passionate about what I'm doing. Scale and complexity are what excite me most at this stage in my career. I guess I'm looking more for a "mission impossible" moment right now.'

It felt good to speak my truth. My need to push myself outside my comfort zone and tackle extreme challenges would never be satisfied in a tame and stable role. I had also grown accustomed to owning a lot of equity and having near full control of decision-making. So, I politely declined the gracious offer.

Then I had the good fortune to connect with Suvir Sujan, a cofounder of Nexus Venture Partners, one of India's largest venture capital (VC) firms. A seasoned entrepreneurial veteran, Suvir was one of the country's e-commerce pioneers. He sold his company to eBay and helped build eBay India. Besides being an impressive business leader and investor, he also had a heart for mentorship and a passion for cultivating and guiding young talent. 'There's a company that I think you might be an ideal candidate for,' he said.

Suvir explained that one of India's leading real estate companies had veered into choppy waters and was looking for a bold, fresh leader who could turn things around. I stopped him midsentence.

'You are too kind,' I said. 'But I don't have a real estate background, Suvir.'

'Yes, but you understand media and tech. They're an online leader.'

'Why in the world would I be suitable for something like that?', I said with a laugh. 'Are you teasing me right now?'

'Totally serious. No joke.'

'You are very nice to think of me. But India has several established leaders in the real estate or technology space—people who are more seasoned leaders in those areas. Besides, a true outsider like me would likely encounter stiff resistance from employees. I can think of a dozen reasons why I'm not the optimal choice for a role like that.'

'Jason, the company I'm talking about is Housing.com. They are one of India's biggest online real estate companies.'

'I'm familiar with them. It's a large operation for sure,' I replied.

'My firm [Nexus] isn't the only investor involved,' said Suvir. 'SoftBank backs them as well. They've invested $100 million.'

The mention of SoftBank piqued my curiosity. I had long admired the entrepreneurial brilliance of their founder and CEO Japanese business mogul Masayoshi Son, sometimes called 'Masa' for short. Not only was Masa one of the world's top billionaires, he had a reputation as a visionary and passionate entrepreneur and investor, one who had been an early backer of companies like Yahoo! and Alibaba, where his $20 million investment, with some additional follow-on investments, is now valued at a staggering $132 billion.

'SoftBank?' I asked. 'As in the company led by Masayoshi Son?'

'Correct,' he said. 'Let me set up a meeting so you can get to know some of their people. What's the worst that could happen? SoftBank is going to be in town soon. If the fit isn't right, at least you will have made some new contacts in the ecosystem.'

If I was serious about pushing my own limits, I needed to follow through and practise what I preached. So, somewhat reluctantly, I agreed that if and when the SoftBank guys were in Mumbai I would meet with them to discuss Housing.com and their CEO search.

My expectations were virtually nonexistent. Still, I'd given my word that I would do an informal interview. So, as is my way, I defaulted to my compulsive need to dive headlong into deep research. I decided to bone up on the Indian real estate market. I set out to learn as much as possible about the sector and Housing.com's positioning within it. Just as I had done when learning bankruptcy laws during the Valiant auction, I scoured reports, case studies, and market data to get to the root of Housing.com's current challenges. I also worked the phones and spoke with industry people that I had a common connect with and many were happy to speak to a now-established entrepreneur.

The odds of SoftBank being interested were extremely low. Nevertheless, I wanted to add value during the eventual interview. If nothing else, I hoped to at least offer intriguing strategic insights or observations they might not have considered, as I was genuinely passionate about solving a complex, multifaceted business problem like this.

The first thing I discovered was just how massive and unorganized the Indian real estate sector was. Even when it came to real estate brokerage firms, at the time, the largest players only had a market share of something approaching 1 per cent. No one had cracked the code on a comprehensive business model that could lock down huge portions of the market. Opportunities abounded. There was enormous headroom to disrupt and capture segments of the industry for those who figured out how to sprint through the labyrinth first and fastest.

Second, many of the reports centred around the lack of trust and transparency in the home-buying process. Lax regulations and shady operators had created a glut of customer horror stories. Families would take an interest in an online home listing, only to show up and be disappointed when the home was not at all as promised.

Overestimating square footages, photos that were nothing like the actual apartment, billing buildings as ready to move in that were still under construction without a clear end date in sight, brokers charging customers different rates, and fake listings—the real estate space was riddled with dissatisfied customers who were tired of being burned on the biggest purchase their family would ever make.

Finally, I researched the most successful real estate brands around the globe and carefully dissected their business models. At the time, China's leading real estate internet portal was a company called SouFun (now known as Fang Holdings Limited). I did a 360-degree drill down on their structure. I also looked at some online real estate players in the US and Europe before determining that the Chinese market was, indeed, the closest parallel to the Indian market.

Whether I would ever use or need any of this research was unclear. Moreover, I was convinced the CEO post at Housing.com was a fantasy. Still, I didn't want to embarrass Suvir by wasting his SoftBank associates' time.

Several days later Suvir called me out of the blue. I remember it distinctly because it was my birthday.

'They're here,' he said.

'Who?' I asked.

'SoftBank. They're in town. Like, right now. I want you to meet them today.'

To celebrate my birthday, I had planned to fulfil the promise I'd made to myself to make the trek to Shirdi. I'd spent years sacrificing my personal life for work. At the risk of appearing uninterested, I didn't feel like putting my life on the backburner for a total long shot.

'Oh, well ... I really appreciate it. But today really isn't a good time. I'm actually leaving town a bit later.'

'Fine. We'll come to you. Please? Jason, they're only here for one day. It will very short, very informal. Just a 30-minute meeting. That's all.'

What was I going to say, 'no'?

When they arrived at the lobby of my apartment complex, Suvir introduced me to SoftBank's then COO, Jonathan Bullock, nicknamed JB for short. British and projecting a military-level of intensity, JB was dry, serious, brilliant, and intimidating. He spit his questions in short, clipped sentences. He then sat expressionless, staring at me like an army general scanning a young private.

'So, what have you done before?' he said flatly.

I spent several minutes telling him about my Valiant journey—the childhood passion, the bankruptcy auction, the trademark wars, building a new team, devising a successful business model, raising rounds of financing, achieving key operating results, awards and strong partnerships, and my exit.

'Okay,' he replied curtly. 'That's fine.'

Gulp.

'Well,' I said trying to quickly shift the conversation to learn more about their situation, 'tell me more about Housing.com.'

JB and Suvir laid out the general corporate overview.

Then I hit JB with a blitzkrieg of questions. 'What is your vision for the company when you first invested and has it changed since then?'

He said they wanted Housing.com to become India's online real estate leader and that vision remains to date.

'What's your view of the current team? What do you think they're doing well? What could be done better?'

He explained there was a team of thousands of people that were a mixture of young talent, underperformers, and a glaring need for strong management and decisive leadership.

'What do you believe the best strategy and business model are?'

He said their goal was for Housing.com to become the Indian equivalent of China's SouFun.

And that's when I made my move.

'So, basically, you're telling me that the strategy and business model still need to be figured out,' I replied. 'Because I've already done some research on SouFun. And here's the thing: they've been forced to change their business model, too. The existential question they face is whether they are going to shift from online to brokerage or do both. There's a channel conflict when you combine both business models, as one serves brokers as customers and the other competes head-on with them; therefore, their revenues and market cap are dropping fast. What I'm saying, JB, is that this is still an unproven strategy and business model and not one that should be emulated just yet.'

A tiny smile formed at the corners of JB's mouth.

'What I'm gathering from this discussion is this,' I continued. 'Housing.com is a company where the strategy and business model both need to be figured out. You need to recruit and hire a new experienced management team. You need to significantly cut costs; in other words, massive restructuring. Next, you need to boost monetization focused on scalable and high-profit margin revenue streams. Right now you're losing millions every month, and that's putting it conservatively. That means changing the entire DNA of the company to make it laser focused on revenues, as opposed to purely product and tech-focused.

'In addition you might need to acquire or merge with another company to spark revenue growth and gain new capabilities overnight. Also, you guys are being trashed across the front pages of major newspapers daily and need to repair the company's battered reputation because it is affecting all aspects of your business. Finally, you need to raise money in the next few months because—and let's just be honest here—you're about to go bankrupt. Housing.com is haemorrhaging cash at an accelerated rate. So much of this rescue needs to happen within six months at the longest.'

JB and Suvir looked at each other and nodded.

'Um, yeah,' JB said wryly, 'that's probably a fair assessment.'

And then, before I could stop myself, the words escaped my mouth.

'Wow, that's really exciting!' I said.

Suvir and JB shot me a look that screamed, *What the hell is wrong with this guy? Is he crazy?* But I sincerely and to my core meant it. Every. Last. Word. It really was a 'mission impossible'. And it would all play out in a media fishbowl with reporters scrutinizing Housing.com CEO's every move, as she or he raced against time to save SoftBank and Nexus's real estate baby from drowning.

By the end of the meeting my interest in the Housing.com CEO position had jumped tenfold. It would be an extreme challenge, the business equivalent of pole vaulting over a skyscraper.

'Jason, it's been a pleasure,' said JB standing up getting ready to leave. 'I like you. I do. As you can imagine, we have many other candidates to meet and consider. In fact, you're actually the first person I've interviewed for Housing.'

'I understand completely,' I said. 'I thoroughly enjoyed the conversation. And thank you for coming and meeting on short notice.'

In the days that followed, I heard around town that SoftBank was interviewing heavy-hitters like the head of Microsoft India and Adobe India—people too seasoned and senior to volunteer to run headlong into a burning building like Housing.

To help organize the CEO search and filter out candidates, Housing had enlisted the large head-hunting firm Spencer Stuart. With Housing.com getting slammed in the Indian media on a daily basis for being on the verge of collapse, the Housing.com investors were in no mood for a risky executive hire.

Spencer Stuart asked me to come in for an interview with their agency's skilled chief Rohit Kale. What then proceeded was the most elaborate and lengthy interview gauntlet I've ever experienced or witnessed. Then SoftBank wanted me to fly to Tokyo, Japan. When I got there, they had me conduct five individual interviews with top executives, including SoftBank's president and CFO of their investment group, Alok Sama, who previously had been a star investment banker at Morgan Stanley, as well as Ming Maa, who went on to become the president of south east Asia's ride sharing superapp powerhouse, Grab.

Between meetings inside their top floor headquarters, I took a restroom break. Standing at the urinal I looked up and realized someone was at the urinal beside mine. I did a quadruple take. It was Masa! Standing at a bathroom urinal was hardly the ideal place to introduce myself and make a strong first impression. So I remained silent with my face staring straight ahead at the wall while I pissed alongside one of the world's richest men. The fact that a man of his power and position didn't have his own restroom humanized Masa in my mind.

Next, Spencer Stuart said that even though SoftBank and Nexus were Housing.com's largest investors in terms of ownership, the company had another dozen or more investors of varying sizes and that I needed to interview with several of them, such as former CEO of media group Network 18 and Viacom 18, Haresh Chawla. At one point I asked the head hunter, 'How many interviews do I have to go through? I understand being thorough, but this is getting a little ridiculous.' They assured me they'd do their best to minimize the remaining number of interviews before proceeding to line up several more.

Next it was on to interviewing with Housing.com's existing management team. I asked SoftBank whether they thought that made sense or whether embattled team members would view any potential incoming chief as a threat. SoftBank said it was important that the next CEO be able to connect with the company's nearly 3,000 employees and blend with the corporate culture while helping it evolve into a more revenue and profit focused company. I was accustomed to being an outsider entering new and unique cultures. I wasn't sure what to expect but hoped for the best.

Housing.com's previous CEO had been fired under controversial circumstances. So they had me interview with the interim CEO who had previously served as COO and a handful of his staff. The team was on the younger side. We shared some jokes before settling in to a relaxed and informal meet-and-greet session. Later that day, JB called me to debrief.

'JB, I really appreciate being considered for Housing's CEO position, but this interview process has been draining. I don't expect the current interim CEO to be excited about recruiting an outsider who may replace him and part of his team,' I said.

JB started laughing.

'What's so funny?' I asked.

'Jason, I'm calling to tell you that the Housing guys really want you.'

'Seriously?'

'Yes. The Housing team really, really wants you.'

'That's wonderful. Thank you for sharing that.'

We then broached the subject of compensation, a topic that hadn't come up in any concrete way throughout the endless rounds of interviewing. He said official numbers and terms would be hammered out later but that the sense was that they were willing to break the budget to get me to sign on for the mission impossible position. Later, Spencer Stuart seemed to confirm that I should expect an aggressive cash and stock options compensation package commensurate with the enormity of the task ahead.

Then they sent me the official offer.

I must have reread the contract a half-dozen times. *I must be misreading this*, I kept saying in my head. *Maybe there's some information in this—some sort of legalese—that I'm not understanding correctly*. I was so flummoxed that I decided to have some trusted business friends look it over as well. But they saw the same thing I did: a CEO offer at literally one-tenth of the pay I'd been led to believe I'd make. I picked up the phone and called the head hunter at Spencer Stuart.

'I'm probably reading this wrong, but this seems to be a fraction of what you told me I could expect,' I said. 'Please tell me I'm missing something here.'

'Jason, unfortunately you are reading it correctly,' said the head hunter. 'I'm really sorry. I mean—truly sorry. I can only advise clients; I can't dictate what they do.'

I decided to speak directly with the SoftBank brass. I was sitting in an airport lounge when I made the call.

'Guys, I have to be honest with you. Is this a joke?' I asked. 'What the hell is going on here? How does this make any sense? I didn't go through all these interviews and fly to Tokyo to get this kind of offer.'

Their basic position was that they disagreed with the head hunter's market-rate salary recommendations. Moreover, they explained, they thought the stock option plan was substantial and sufficient. Thankfully I knew quite a bit about the slippery world of stock option plans, as I had designed an innovative stock option plan for Valiant to ensure everyone could share in value creation.

It's something every young Indian entrepreneur must understand. Many companies will dangle the lure of equity in the face of hot new talent. 'You'll own a piece of the company,' they'll say. 'You'll be on the ground floor of an empire that may one day make you millions.' In some cases, that may be true. But in many cases the stock option plans are so 'employer-friendly' that they aren't worth the paper they're printed on.

Why? Several reasons. First, according to Indian law, if you work somewhere for less than one year, your stock options are worth zero. (That can also be the case in the US, depending upon the contract language.) So if you leave on, say, the 364th day after you joined the company, you get zilch.

Second, depending on the contract specifics, there's often a clause in the stock option agreement that dictates that you have to exercise what's vested within three months of leaving the company. If you can't cash out within those three months, you lose it all. The problem with that is if you exercise it, you have to find a buyer to sell your relatively small number of shares—something very hard to do for a private company.

What happens is that the tax authorities see it as you gaining an asset; it's not different from you gaining cash, even though you received none, and you have to pay tax on that. And of course the overarching issue with stock options is that they can be priced so high that the chances of them being worth much is slim. So you have to assess what price you're getting in at and also the number of shares you're receiving relative to the total number of shares.

All that said, let me be crystal clear: I believe our country's nascent ecosystem is akin to Silicon Valley before it became Silicon Valley, or China before it became the economic behemoth that it is today. *Now* is the best time to plant your seeds in gaining experience, building relationships, and gaining equity, whether by entering an existing company or acquiring founder shares. India is bursting with opportunity. I see it everywhere, every day. Even if we only realize *half* the promise on the horizon, that's going to be an empire of value creation. So now is the time to make your mark, not when our market is fully matured and cash and equity allotments are firmly dried in cement.

Bottom line: stock option plans must be reviewed and negotiated carefully.

Now, when it came to the Housing.com stock option plan, I knew it was flawed and not nearly as attractive as it might first appear. I was direct with the SoftBank execs about that, too. They agreed with my points and said reconstituting their stock option plan was one of the many things they wanted me to work on as CEO. They also conceded that there weren't many stock options left. They said they could give me more later. Then, after a long pause, I made my counter offer.

'Look, guys, I get it. I'll tell you what. Here's what I'm prepared to do. I'm willing to dive in and roll up my sleeves. I meant what I said during that first meeting. I find the enormity of the task ahead exciting. But you need to promise me that in a few months' time, you will get the market data and calculate what the right amounts should be. If you will honour that, I will take this on. Then, after you see my value add, you'll do the right thing and adjust this to levels that are more than fair.' They seemed relieved and elated but added a new twist to the process.

To my surprise, Housing.com's investors now wanted me to serve in the number two slot as Chief Business Officer (CBO) as a sort of post-interview interview! It turned out to be a wise move on their part; the CBO role allowed me to gain trust as an outsider and get my arms around the totality of the instability and deficiencies. It was also an ideal way for me to get my lay of the land quickly. In effect, they were giving me a 'trial run' for the CEO role, a high-profile risky leadership post for investors to fill. After three months, I thought I passed the test.

But before they named me Housing.com's CEO, the board said I need to interview (*another* interview!) with SoftBank's publicly anointed successor to Masa, business legend Nikesh Arora. He had long been a personal inspiration of mine. An Indian immigrant in the US, Nikesh had worked his way to become Google's CBO. After Sergey Brin, Larry Page, and Eric Schmidt, he was Google's next most senior executive. From there he'd gone on to become SoftBank's president and the highest paid executive in the world.

When I arrived for my meeting with Nikesh, I was first unexpectedly interviewed by Liane Hornsey. A former senior Google executive who later became Uber's human resources (HR) chief, Liane asked smart, probing questions. She was passionate about teamwork and seemed pleased that I expressed the same philosophy.

Nikesh was running late. I was asked to wait for him outside what I was told was a 'bunker' in the Bharti SoftBank building in Delhi. Apparently, the structure was an underground soundproof room. Inside, Nikesh was deeply engrossed in a government auction. Outside the bunker was a room overflowing with Japanese analysts frantically chirping on phones and tapping computer keyboards while monitoring the auction. Suddenly, the bunker door flung open. Nikesh emerged. The room stopped.

'Sorry for running so late,' Nikesh said. 'Every few seconds the bid fluctuated, costing me millions of dollars. So I needed to handle it personally.'

'Did you win?' I asked.

'I did.'

'Congratulations!'

'Actually I think I clearly overpaid. But that's okay. All part of a bigger strategy.'

Nikesh looked me over.

'I've heard about you,' he said. 'Let's take a ride and talk.'

We made our way to his black Mercedes and got in the car. JB joined us.

'Sometimes the most memorable meetings happen when I ride like this,' Nikesh explained.

His questions were airtight and tough. He had a reputation for shredding lazy logic. He said he was sceptical of supporting a troubled company. I did my best to convince him otherwise and said I believed in the company and the cause. We then debated key points, as he asked me about the market, Housing's competitors, business models and a path to success.

I thought my answers were strong. He seemed to appreciate my point of view, but it was clear Nikesh was like a chess grandmaster; he was always three steps ahead. I found his foresight and panoramic vision inspiring. And he was right: it was, indeed, a memorable meeting.

With Nikesh's blessing in hand, I was named Housing's new CEO.

The deal was sealed. Just in my early thirties, I would become the CEO of a company with 3,000 employees, offices in 30 cities, cratering market share, press coverage that was the thing PR nightmares were made of, and just a couple of months' worth of operating cash before the whole thing went up in flames.

Insane as it may sound, I was ecstatic.

Housing.com was burning down. I wanted to assemble and lead the team that could extinguish the flames and turn the company around.

8

Harness the Power of Focus

SMART PEOPLE WHOM I respect thought I had lost my mind.

'Jason, why are you doing this?' a Harvard Business professor and one of India's leading real estate investors asked me when I told him I accepted the CEO post at Housing.com. 'You don't need the money. The company has a messy history; you may not even know all the skeletons in the closet. It's on the verge of bankruptcy.'

'Well,' I told him, 'believe it or not I like the mission and the people behind it, the team of investors.'

'I'm sure they're all great,' he said. 'But this is India. You could go to jail!'

'I appreciate the concern. But I'm willing to do whatever it takes to help them and save Housing.com.'

He wasn't the only person who cautioned me about becoming the CEO of a major company in crisis; several others did as well. But if there's any upside to business crises, it is that they force you to focus like few things can. That was certainly the case with my tenure at the helm of Housing.com.

Right out of the gate, for the first couple of weeks, I set up hour-long meetings with key individuals and small groups. These relaxed sessions were meant to build meaningful bonds, foster trust, and get an on-the-ground perspective of what employees—at all levels and positions—saw as the company's challenges and opportunities. I wanted to create a discursive space where people felt comfortable and safe bringing up negatives. During the sessions I worked hard to maintain direct eye contact and listen actively.

I modified my messaging and delivery depending on the department and region of each talk. For example, while giving a talk in the north at an office like Noida in UP, I would be louder and more forceful in my delivery, compared to Chennai, where I would be more soft-spoken, tailoring each message to the local subculture.

I used a similar approach when I spoke to the product tech teams. These employees tended to be more excited about innovation than money, the most educated in the company, and very logic-driven in their thinking. So I focused more on company impact than financial results, and included more objective data than if I spoke to, say, the operations team.

Then, after each session, I made copious notes and recorded every detail while employee reflections were still fresh in my memory. A constellation of patterns soon emerged. If several people all said the same thing in different ways, I knew that problem was an institutional fact.

In addition to holding my sessions, I also sat in on regular team meetings. That's where I realized how chaotic things were. During my first management meeting, several of the younger staff were screaming, shouting, and fighting with one another. I sat quietly, doing my best to divorce the emotion from the underlying issues animating the outbursts. The key was keeping an open mind and avoiding forming any immediate assumptions. Instead, I needed to listen. And not that phony corporate head nodding listening. Deep focus listening—the kind that extracts key learnings. Executives who take the time to talk to fifty or more employees at all levels of the organizational chart and keep an open mind will be amazed at what they'll learn.

Because I was the only one doing these kinds of sessions, I ended up with the clearest picture of what was going on. I'd talk to junior salespersons and say, 'Hey, how's it going? How's your experience been here at Housing.com? Who've you been selling to? What works? What doesn't? What do you think we can do better? And how?'

These weren't earth-shattering questions. They were ways to make people feel comfortable reporting information—both good and bad. I wanted the team to know their ideas and input truly mattered, that they weren't just being patted on the head and placated but listened to as respected colleagues with important insights worthy of consideration.

Immediately, I was apprised of several 'red alert' situations, challenges far beyond those initially reported. The most immediate and harrowing of these problems was the big, glaring reality staring Housing.com in the face: it didn't just have a murky business model, it had *no* business model. There had never been a clear focus, and without that the most elemental pieces of business often get ignored.

No one had done the deep research based on models, data, and metrics to build a profitable plan. Instead, Housing.com was a hodge-podge of stratagems without real performance metrics to determine whether they were producing value. Thousands of employees all scurrying around doing their best to turn a profit, but without any organized, centralized system in place to make strategic, data-driven decisions to maximize value. Housing needed a clear business model—and fast. So I settled on an unorthodox method to develop one.

I hopped on a jet and flew to China—the real estate market that was the most similar to India's. I stayed for over a week. There, SoftBank set me up with numerous meetings—many lasting several hours—with CEOs and executives of China's top real estate companies, including one lengthy and invaluable session with SouFun's founder Vincent Mo.

Compiling secondary research was helpful, but gaining those next-level insights could only come from meeting the founder one-on-one and asking him the big questions. 'Why did you change your business model? Why did you add this revenue stream? What are the biggest hurdles going from online to offline?' Those were the kinds of insights annual reports and case studies could never provide.

In all my meetings in China every question I asked was aimed at pulling back the curtain in search of a successful business model. The Chinese real estate professionals I spoke to were candid and kind. Each of their companies had all started at different stages. Some were solely online, in essence tech companies that didn't get involved with the nuts and bolts of property, land, and building, but were simply online portals featuring home and apartment listings that made their money selling ads. Others were brick and mortar. But no matter what stage each company began in, over several years, they all had converged to some form of a single model.

Here's how it worked. The online platform would capture customer information. Then a living, breathing real estate agent would reach out to the customer. From there, they would shepherd the homebuyer offline, with in-person meetings and visits to homes for sale, while collecting a brokerage fee. Finally, on top of this process, they cross-sold customers home insurance and home loans to create what we call a 'full stack'—meaning an end-to-end customer service—real estate business model.

Creating a comprehensive, one-stop-shop home-buying experience with a combination of technology and real humans you can trust—that was the path that produced large revenues, profits, and growth. Every major Chinese real estate company making money was doing it this way.

The other thing that became clear during my China meetings was how quick and easy it was for real estate players to fall for false and misleading metrics. For example, on paper, it may appear to make sense to offer and promote rental properties, such as town homes or apartments. But often that would simply tie up salespeople on tiny transactions. Worse, it might cannibalize a potential homebuyer and turn them into a renter instead.

Finally, the most profitable companies in China weren't necessarily those that had branches and offices in tons of cities; instead, they had focused on the core locations that comprised the bulk of their business. Better to provide superior customer service in a handful of highly profitable cities rather than spotty service in many cities. What's more, having fledgling branches strewn across the country only eroded brand equity and torched mountains of cash.

Put another way, it wasn't just inefficient, it was a financial cost that could sink a company.

This successful model was very different than anything we had in India. At the time, the whole Indian market for digital advertising in real estate was $200 million (which included Google and Facebook ad spending), with two entrenched organized players in Magic Bricks and 99 Acres. The Indian real estate brokerage market back then was $7 billion, with no major organized player. Now here's where it gets tricky.

Based on our research, being an online real estate-only player required being number one or, at worst, number two in your market due to network effects, in order to gain considerable market share, leverage from buyers and sellers to raise their prices and your profits to create a valuable company. In this scenario, as played out in most markets around the world, the winner takes all or most of the market and value creation, making it a risky high-stakes zero sum game.

Like most Indian real estate companies, Housing had basically been a tech play—an online listing service that generated most revenue through advertising and premium listing placements. In other words, it was a strictly online company. The successful Chinese companies had transitioned from solely online or solely offline to online-to-offline. If we could do the same, we would be the first in India to do so at scale.

Flying back home to India from China, I felt invigorated. I knew what needed to happen and was confident it would work. The Chinese model was proven. This was no time to try some experimental, risky model that had never been tested. For all its challenges, the Housing.com brand was well-known. Moreover, it was a company with 3,000 employees and over $100 million raised. Put simply, this was no longer a start-up—real livelihoods and investments were all on the line. The Chinese real estate model was a winner. SoftBank agreed with my assessment.

Still, even the best plan requires the right teammates to execute it. From the outset, I set out to attract and hire world-class management talent. As CEO, I needed an executive team with the level of expertise, skills, and experience commensurate with a company of Housing's size. That's exactly what I got—and then some. In fact, I will go so far as to say that the group we assembled was one of the most gifted and experienced management teams the Indian internet space has ever seen.

JB created a detailed scoring system that we used to rate potential hires. I then spent hours with candidates drilling down on how their minds worked, why they'd made the choices they'd made at key decision points in their careers, and the skills they possessed. Hiring the right team would be everything.

The choice of whom to hire is axial. That one decision has a cascading effect into all the future moves that employees will later make and implement. What's more, when you hire a great manager, they will, in turn, likely hire good people, too. As a holistic business leader who believes deeply in teamwork, I knew how critical these hires would prove.

The team we assembled did not disappoint. I hired a new chief marketing officer, Nikhil Rungta, who was the founding CMO of a tiny company you may have heard of, called Google India. He was one of the rarest of talents, someone with deep offline and online marketing experience in India. How did I get him to agree to join Housing.com? I told him, 'This is a rare opportunity to play a key role in one of the most challenging but exciting turnarounds. You're a marketing veteran. I'm not. I am a holistic business leader. I'm going to rely on you for the marketing and only guide you with some key goals and metrics to meet. But I'm going to give you a lot of trust and freedom in your domain to manoeuvre.'

Put simply, I told him I respected him too much to micromanage him. Instead, I would guide his goals and empower and equip him with the resources needed to achieve them. He liked that.

I hired a new CFO, Mani Rangarajan. Mani's previous job? Serving as the chief of staff to the president and CFO of Yahoo! He was, hands down, one of the most experienced CFOs in the Indian internet space. And now I'd hired him straight from Silicon Valley.

I hired Nandini Mehta as our general counsel. Previously, she had been a partner at J. Sagar Associates (JSA), one of the country's best law firms. Before that, she had worked for legendary Bollywood producer and Indian cable pioneer Ronnie Screwvala. A total pro and whip smart, Nandini was the consummate professional and a legal eagle second to none.

I hired Vivek Jain as my chief product technology officer. He had been the head of Reliance Jio's digital media business where he helped build a Netflix for India and reported directly to Mukesh Ambani. As if all that weren't enough, before that he'd held senior roles at Amazon and Google.

Then there was the street-smart executive I inherited as CHRO, Ajay Nair, a former COO of Omkar real estate developers with a high tolerance for navigating through the rough and dangerous waters Housing.com was sailing through. Also, former Bain strategy consultant Abhishek Hota, a talented executive with Housing.com during the early days whom I promoted to be my Chief of Staff due to his institutional knowledge, strategic mind, and deep understanding of internal relationship dynamics. Finally, I brought on Dilip Tuli, a rock star KPMG consultant who had worked with me on prior deals, and whom I appointed to be vice president of operations and strategic initiatives due to his extensive experience working on the mechanics of due diligence for deals.

Collectively, they were the dream team, a brain trust of talent that represented the best of the best. I was humbled and blessed to have them at my side. No turnaround is ever the work of one person; teamwork is the lifeblood of focus and execution. I can say with confidence that the remarkable turnaround Housing.com experienced was because these and many other seasoned professionals chose to join me on one of the most breakneck business adventures I will likely ever encounter.

I worked hard to foster a collaborative team culture, one where each person's expertise was leveraged as we iterated and innovated. I'd set the key responsibility areas (KRAs) and key performance indicators (KPIs) for each division or team, and then lean on my management team to optimize and execute. Often meetings would run until two or three o'clock in the morning. We were racing against time to save a company. All the while I would ask the team questions. Are these the right metrics? Are these the right targets? My goal was to build a machine where all the pieces came together to maximize each person's talents.

With my information-gathering sessions providing valuable employee insights and my dream management team firmly in place, it was now time to do the hard and brutal work of resuscitating Housing.com. We focused our energies on turning the business model we'd gleaned from studying the Chinese market into an operational plan, complete with a detailed calendar filled with benchmarks and targets. Nothing like it had ever been tried in India. JB pushed and pushed until the operating plan was razor sharp.

No matter how well-crafted the plan was, I knew I was likely to encounter internal resistance. In a company with thousands of employees, being a CEO can sometimes be a little like being a politician of a small village. You find yourself lobbying, persuading, debating, and hopefully inspiring your thousands of 'constituents' that you have a strong vision and plan that puts the village's best interests on a path towards success.

But unlike a politician who gets to lead during a season of prosperity and peace, I'd been hired as a turnaround man, a CEO sprinting against time to rescue a company in freefall. Turnarounds always involve extremely painful, gut-wrenching cost-cutting and restructuring that typically takes the form of layoffs. That's why they're called turnarounds—business crises that demand extreme measures to save a company from ruin or collapse.

Being a 'popular' or 'beloved' leader in such circumstances is unrealistic. Instead, my goal was to implement our business model in the most respectful and humane manner possible in order to save the jobs of the employees who remained and hopefully create new ones as Housing battled back from the brink.

But there was no escaping the fact that the restructuring would be fraught with difficulty and potentially even physical danger.

~

A CEO's decision to let employees go is one of the most painful they ever have to make. During my eighteen-month tenure as Housing.com's CEO, it was for me.

Most entrepreneurs have heard the old adage 'heavy is the head that wears the crown'. But you can't really learn it until you live it. Like a surgeon, business leaders in a time of crisis are often forced to perform painful procedures in order to save a business and protect the jobs of the employees who remain. When a business is near death, band-aids won't do.

After extensive research and calculations by the executive management team, we discovered that the original cash projections of six remaining months of capital had been too rosy. The real number was two months. Housing was burning millions of dollars every month. In addition, they had a large number of unpaid accrued liabilities. Thankfully, we were able to successfully negotiate them down or settle them to save the company ₹40 crore. But even with that, we needed to cut costs by nearly 80 per cent or face extinction. That meant sliming our locations, spread across thirty cities, down to the most profitable eight locations by laying off nearly 1,000 employees.

On the day of the layoffs, my staff requested that I remain offsite for security purposes. We had a full HR team in place to assist each employee with the necessary paperwork and to help them with job placements elsewhere. We also had prepared generous severance plans, healthcare, and did our best to be as fair and respectful as possible. Still, no matter how well and humanely we tried to make the process, the heartbreaking reality was that I was about to inform 1,000 people they no longer had a job.

The communication team and I had crafted a company-wide email announcing the decision. Now, sitting in my apartment, it was up to me to press send. I sat staring at the email, reading it over and over while my stomach churned. Finally, around 10:30 a.m., I hit send. Here is what it said:

From: Jason Kothari <jason.kothari@housing.com>
To: Everyone <everyone@housing.com>

Subject: Focus, Efficiency & Letting Great People Go

Dear Team,

Housing has always believed in looking up and moving fast. A lot has been achieved in these last few years but going forward, we believe a focused approach is necessary to win the real estate opportunity in India and create a very successful company.

In order to meet the above goals, we are making some important strategic changes to the company strategy & organization:

1. **Establish a single and unified company focus on the largest and most lucrative real estate category (i.e. BUY-SELL)**
2. **Attain a sustainable cost structure by improving operational efficiencies**

3. **Retain or build key capabilities for competitive advantage and future market leadership in BUY-SELL**

We have built one of the best Rent platforms but unfortunately the market offers limited financial potential. There is also no clear business model anywhere in the world that has successfully monetized Rent, while there is a proven business model in BUY-SELL that has successfully created numerous large companies globally.

At a time in the economy where capital is limited, we are hard pressed but need to allocate 100% of our resources & mindshare on winning the BUY-SELL market. In addition, we need to be much more efficient with our resources.

I'm writing this to you with mixed feelings—on one hand, I couldn't be more excited about our new focused strategy and what it could mean for Housing's future; on the other hand, I have a heavy heart that we will need to let some of our talented colleagues and friends go work elsewhere ... nevertheless, I am confident this will be better for all parties in the long-run. Housing will get its chance to succeed in a big way, and they will succeed in their own way, elsewhere, where they are needed more.

A right decision can sometimes be difficult, but it doesn't change the fact that it is right. It is a right decision like this that can propel this potentially great company. We don't want to let this chance go, it might never come back.

We are in this together, and I am here by your side to help in any way possible. Please reach out to me, any other member of the management or HR team for anything at all. Don't hesitate. That's why we're here.

Regards,
Jason

Throughout the day I received twenty-minute updates via phone, WhatsApp, and email. The vast majority of the individuals affected were disappointed but understanding. Many even expressed gratitude for our assistance. Still, a few took the news much harder.

I received a frantic call from an HR team member who said one person was expressing suicidal thoughts. I instructed them to send a manager to his home right away. Thankfully, after extensive conversations, the former employee calmed down and we were able to help him. But the scary incident was a grim example of how difficult restructuring can be.

A small contingent of disgruntled employees took their grievances to a local politician. Soon, the word on the street was that a political leader had threatened violence against me and the management team and was mobilizing a mob to protest, storm the office, and spark a violent clash—all with the media cameras rolling.

Given that there have been incidents of management being injured or killed during similar large-scale restructurings, the investors huddled and hired the famous detective agency Pinkerton to provide a private security team on the premises. Most of the security professionals were undercover in plainclothes to remain invisible across multiple offices. Other than the investors, I was the only person to know about the secret security team so as not alarm or compromise employees' safety. Throughout, my goal as CEO was to keep my people safe, remain calm and focused, and do everything possible to do the restructuring as humanely as possible.

That respectful treatment also extended to the young and talented Housing.com cofounders. Ten out of the twelve of them remained when I joined the company. Most lacked clearly defined roles. Many of the investors and management felt they were potentially disruptive to the company's transformation; they wanted me to either keep them in the dark or let them all go. I refused to do either. As I mentioned before, my philosophy towards founders is different than many.

Instead of kicking them to the curb I met with them on a bi-weekly basis and gave them transparent status updates. I also encouraged them to take their time to find roles that made sense for the company and themselves and assured them we would continue paying them until then. Downsizing and restructuring weren't going to be easy, but I felt it was important to be respectful towards the cofounders' roles in creating and building Housing in the early stages.

Within five days, the process was complete. I assured the remaining 2,000 staff members that the painful layoffs were over; they could now rest easy as we went about the hard work of transforming Housing.com from an online to offline real estate company.

From its inception, Housing.com had been a tech company with a bunch of passionate, smart engineers who were handed a boatload of money and told to do whatever they wanted with it. Those tech engineers built a dazzling, beautiful digital platform dripping with all the aspects of real estate one could ever want. But this, 'everything and the kitchen sink' approach, had no strategic business plan underneath it to grow revenues. There were tons of cool, shiny features … that made little business sense. The trickle of revenue the company did create came through selling banner ads to home brokers and large building developers.

As I mentioned, many Indian real estate customers had grown tired of fake or misleading low-quality listings that frequently proved to be little more than a bait and switch. It was a glaring consumer pain point. To overcome this perception, we needed to differentiate ourselves from competitors by offering the highest quality and most accurate listings possible.

After conducting deep market research our senior management team concluded that our verified listing feature could be the difference to help us stand out from the crowd. By having a huge field force on the ground, Housing.com employees were able to physically verify the many data points and details of property listings. That meant when we showed a home on Housing.com, you could be certain that details, such as square footage, number of rooms, price, lot size, appliances, were all accurate.

Some of our investors groused, 'Jason, why should Housing.com confirm every listing themselves? This is expensive. No other company does this. We need to get rid of that.' Indeed, having to pay hundreds of people in our field force to fan out across India and do the grunt work of verifying every detail was a significant business expense. But the data clearly showed that trust was the core value customers craved in the home-buying process. So, with online real estate guru Simon Baker serving as a sounding board to keep our efforts on the right track, my executive team and I fought to make it one of the cornerstones of our brand.

Another major decision was to offer sellers and developers a strong return on investment for their ad dollars by guaranteeing a certain number of leads when running ads. Even though we were working to transition and evolve the offline side of our real estate business, we still needed to generate online revenue quickly to hopefully make the case to investors to give us even more.

To give our monetization efforts a steroid shot, we wanted to further differentiate ourselves from competitors like Magic Bricks and 99 Acres. After all, both had been in business ten years longer than we had. That meant they had deeper relationships and brand awareness. If we were going to win over advertisers, we would need to offer them something special.

With those companies and ours, homesellers would basically buy a banner ad or a 'native' ad (one that's blended into the list of homes so as not to look and feel like an ad), and hope for the best. Our engineers, however, created an algorithm that determined a set number of buyer leads per ad buy.

This meant a building developer could, say, spend $500 on an ad package, knowing he or she would receive a predetermined number of phone calls or emails from interested homebuyers—a clear value proposition that helped us generate quick infusions of revenue as we built out the offline 'full stack' side of the business.

In short, we could now go to building developers and say, 'We're not going to waste your time or money. You pay on a performance basis.' That allowed us to forge great relationships with major building companies and to regain credibility and trust.

As we racked up wins, we went on offense with our PR. One of my early edicts had been no more reactionary, defensive communications. Instead, we would promote positive brand messages through a proactive approach to public relations. Every single week, no matter how large or small the development, I had our communication team blast out press releases that left a sweet taste in readers' mouths. You either control brand perceptions or get controlled by them. For too long Housing.com had done the latter and paid a massive price. What entrepreneurs have to understand is that perceptions become reality.

Negative brand perceptions are corrosive to the leader's ability to recruit, retain, and motivate employees. People want to know their work matters—that they work for a company that's going places. Moreover, brand perceptions have a huge role in encouraging or discouraging business partnerships, mergers, and raising money from investors. You don't create positive perceptions from a single press release or news article. You do so by hammering a core message. Every. Single. Week.

For our efforts, we were nominated for and won leading communication awards for crisis management. We also became the most popular social media brand for Indian real estate. But far more important than accolades were the results strong communication produced. Our investors were pleased and hungry for more. They asked me to aggressively evangelize our company's wins through media television appearances and interviews. I tapped into my reservoir of communication confidence and took to the airwaves to champion our success story.

As I mentioned, the core value of customer 'trust' was one of our 'north stars' we used to guide communications. If we claimed to be the 'most trusted' online real estate company in India, we needed to demonstrate that. How? Not by *claiming* to be trusted, but *showing* we were trusted. So when we hired, say, a top manager, we did a victory lap in the press. The meta-message of course was that if a top former Google executive believes in Housing.com enough to come aboard, customers should also. It paid off. In fact, LinkedIn named us the ninth most sought after employer in the country, and this despite all the restructuring we were forced to do.

Likewise, when revenue growth began to climb or website traffic spiked, we made sure people knew about it by placing those stories in the business press. Doing so conveyed to homebuyers that other customers were placing increasing levels of trust in us. We bartered expired media credit—essentially zero cost—for a highly coveted Indian Premier League (IPL) television ad slot that normally would cost millions and managed to reach 200 million people.

The same thing we were doing externally we did internally. Boosting employee morale isn't about doing a bunch of cheesy rah-rah happy talk. Instead, it comes through positive but meaningful communication with employees. Sometimes I would do that at a company-wide level, through emails highlighting achievements, such as a large new developer, customer, or a jump in revenues. But one of the most effective methods I implemented was to continue using the town hall format with smaller groups. I wouldn't compromise on that.

'You know what?' I'd say to my executive team. 'I don't want to speak to 300 people at once. I want it personal. It's more impactful and effective that way. So instead of one dry talk to 300, let's do ten meetings with thirty people apiece.' They'd be like, 'Are you crazy? You're going to do ten meetings when you could knock it out in one?' I told them it would be fine; I'd just break them up into smaller increments (sort of like I did with my extreme push-up exercises in college). Yes, it took more time that way. Literally ten times as much time, to be exact. But it also made ten times the impact. I'd always reserve ample time for questions and answers. With thirty people, everyone knew you were focused on them, not a sea of faces in a crowd. When you're trying to steer a massive ship and get 2,000 people to all row in the same direction with drive and spirit, it's critical that they feel the leader's energy and hear the logic and passion behind the plan being implemented.

All this is not to suggest that I was always successful in convincing and persuading every single employee that our business model was the best path to pursue. Indeed, one of the most vital decisions I made as Housing's CEO also proved to be one of the most controversial among our employees.

That involved my decision to do away with every vertical that didn't involve buying and selling homes. That meant getting rid of some divisions that were popular with our employees. Chief among these was the rentals vertical. Shutting down the rent offerings meant we could take hundreds of employees and shift their focus to doing deals that were infinitely more lucrative. Put simply, instead of wasting a Housing.com employee's time on a customer wanting to rent a $500 a month apartment, that same employee could now focus on closing a sale on a $500,000 home.

The math was undeniable. In fact, one of the big takeaways I'd picked up on my China sojourn was that all the biggest players had also done the math on rent and had come to the same conclusion: the numbers didn't work. Then my executive team crunched our own numbers and discovered they were right.

Housing.com had become known more for rent than buying and selling. Most of the team had spent far more time on the rent side of the platform, than on the buying and selling side. Younger employees could relate to it more, as young people who rented and couldn't afford to buy. What's more, 80 per cent of our mind-share resources were focused on rent even though the revenue model was poor. So when I made the decision that it was time to close rent down, it sparked an extremely controversial and contentious battle inside our company.

I knew it was a debate I needed to have in order to win over as many adherents internally as I could. So when the objections came fast and furious, I welcomed them.

'How dare you say that? What are you talking about? Rent is our best product! Ask anyone in the market! Besides, 50 per cent of people visit our website looking for rent. That synergistically then leads them to check out buying instead. It's the most popular part of our entire platform!'

Then it was my turn.

'Most popular in what sense? You said a lot of our visits are to the rent section but end up in the buying and selling section. But have you looked at the data? Because I have. Let's take a look at it together. Only 10 per cent of the people coming in through rent click over into buying and selling. But everyone in our company assumes it's 70 per cent. But you see it's not. That's a myth we've allowed to become ingrained in our thinking.'

Then I laid out the case not for just the direct costs of running the rent division but the indirect costs as well. I explained that shifting the hundreds of people working on rent to the buying and selling division was infinitely more lucrative. For most, these arguments and data points were enough to get them to buy into the plan. But for others, they still wanted to believe that there must be some way we could have made money off their beloved rent vertical. I didn't outright disagree with them. Instead, I explained that the time for innovation and experimentation with exotic approaches to monetization is not when you have a couple months of cash in the bank and investors are telling you they're about to shut down the business.

I estimate that roughly 80 per cent of our workforce came to understand the sound business sense behind my controversial decision to end rent and focus on buying and selling homes. I was okay with that. I knew the decision was the fulcrum that would lift revenues, attract mergers, and entice deep-pocketed investors. Would I have liked unanimous support from my employees? Sure. But leadership isn't a popularity contest. Executives who need to be adored, or who avoid unpopular but necessary decisions, do so to their company's detriment.

I was reminded of just how true that statement is during a SoftBank investors meeting with Masa and Nikesh that took place towards the latter part of my Housing.com tenure. They were doing business-update meetings with their Indian CEOs and founders from Hike, Ola, Snapdeal, and others all seated around a large table at The Oberoi in Gurgaon. During one leader's update they reported that they had to ask ten people to go and that it had been difficult. Nikesh stopped him midsentence.

'You think that's difficult,' said Nikesh putting his hand on my shoulder. 'Jason here had to let 1,000 people go from a mess he didn't even create. He has every reason to complain, you don't.'

Later, I delivered my update to Masa and Nikesh and they seemed impressed and pleased with how we had restructured the company, focused on the big business problem, and generated a sizable improvement in results so quickly.

What I came to understand was that Housing.com was much more than just money to the investors. It was a blemish on their otherwise sterling reputations. Everywhere they went around the world, regardless of the venue or discussion, they were asked in interviews how they had screwed up so badly with Housing.com. To finally have real results and a positive brand story to tell was a welcome reprieve.

To their credit, the investors also saw to it that my compensation—left in limbo when I accepted the CEO position—was eventually corrected. I was told it was the highest compensation given to a CEO in the Indian internet space, including ownership at the level of a company founder.

When they saw the financial and operating results, Nikesh and the other investors agreed that my compensation was justified. Even though it was no longer about money for me at this stage of my career, having the investors thank me profusely for helping save the company made all the trials and tribulations worth it.

In the end the business strategy that my team and I implemented during my eighteen months as CEO, worked. In fact, it was so successful that Harvard Business School later created a case study on our Housing.com turnaround for one of their classes and asked me to come speak at the university on how we achieved it.

The numbers tell the story. Housing.com revenues jumped 400 per cent, making us India's fastest growing online real estate company. Our costs plunged 70 per cent, making us one of the lowest cost companies in the entire sector. Demand surged as well. We had a 215 per cent growth in monthly website visits, which made

Housing.com the most popular platform for buying and selling homes in all of India. That popularity, in turn, drove supply higher.

Specifically, we had a 460 per cent growth in Housing.com listings, making us the largest selection of resale homes and new, verified projects. Our media mentions generated a greater media share of voice than all competitors combined. Best of all, the tonality of the coverage was now predominantly positive. And of course with numbers like these and a positive brand image, SoftBank pumped fresh infusions of funding into Housing.com.

Somewhere around this time, I received a message on LinkedIn from Kanika, the same girl from Shaadi.com who 'interviewed' me some five years ago. She mentioned she had moved back to Mumbai and would like to meet. I was surprised and intrigued to find out why she would message me now. During our call, I asked, 'Why am I hearing from you only after so many years?'

She hesitated and said, 'Hmm, I got a bit busy ... I don't know if you are still single but if you are, I am very interested.' I couldn't stop chuckling about the dating realities of an entrepreneur's journey. And yes, I said 'NO!'

On the business side, merger offers came rolling in as well. Merger and acquisition (M&A) deals all come with their own unique set of challenges and opportunities. Enacting our business model of taking Housing.com from an online real estate business to an offline company meant we'd either have to build it ourselves, buy it, or partner with someone with proven offline capabilities. Without the time or money to do the first two, we went with the latter approach, which meant entering into M&A discussions.

Eight out of ten pan-India companies in the real estate services space, including all seven offline-focused companies, were interested in a merger with Housing.com. The process was like speed-dating in New York City (no joke, that experience genuinely helped me in business!). I met a different CEO for breakfast, another for lunch, and still another for dinner, all in the same day to discuss a possible partnership with each one.

As I met with leaders from companies like HDFC Realty, India Infoline, Square Yards, PropTiger, India Homes, India Property, JLL Residential, I made an effort to build or rebuild relationships with their CEOs and investors which had become strained under the previous management team. I was pleasantly surprised to learn that all of these companies admired the turnaround work Housing had done and that every one of them made offers to merge with us.

The best M&A advice I can give you is to focus on trust and transparency. Even if all the business synergies are there, without trust, it won't work. On the flip side, if there aren't clear business synergies, but there is trust and a willingness to collaborate, people can find ways to create value together. In our case, we were honest about our strengths and weaknesses, and offered data on both.

The largest valuation one of the parties offered was $150 million—a handsome number, given the fact that eighteen months ago we were on the verge of going out of business, and also more than the amount investors had put in. But our investors and I really wanted the best partner long-term. In the end, we merged with News Corp-backed PropTiger in a deal that created India's largest digital real estate company valued at $350 million and most well capitalized with $55 million for business growth.

It was important for myself and PropTiger CEO Dhruv Agarwala to spend time together over many subsequent meetings. Getting to know each other helped foster and strengthen bonds of trust, to ensure a proper fit between corporate cultures and business synergies. Having handled multiple deals during and after serving as Valiant CEO, I knew which places to focus on and what pressure points to work through to help forge a deal.

The other factor in our merger, of course, was News Corp, PropTiger's backer.

News Corp is the largest online real estate player in the world. That meant we knew they were most likely to add value as an investor and long-term partner. Because of their size and brand power, they negotiated hard. Their original deal was for $150 million valuation for Housing.com, matching the highest we received (or a 1:1 equity swap ratio that later became 1:3 in their favour when they agreed to infuse an additional $50 million).

It was not a cash sale but a merger, as all shareholders would continue in the combined company, and hence choosing the right company was more important than just valuation alone. Bottom line: M&A deals should not be driven solely by valuation, but rather by a host of variables including trust, cultural fit, and business synergies, which must all be considered.

During the merger negotiations, real life came crashing down. My maternal grandmother, whom we called Ba, had to be hospitalized. Things were touch and go. I was twenty minutes away from the hospital, so I began making regular visits when my work and travel schedule allowed. While trying to resolve some issues on the possible Housing.com–PropTiger merger, I received a call from my mother. Ba had just passed away. I wanted to be there more than anything, to be by her side, and I couldn't believe that in the midst of the work, I had lost the opportunity.

It made me question whether the sacrifice was worth it. CEOs and entrepreneurs must make immense sacrifices to fulfil their responsibilities. Often those sacrifices are made with no thanks or acknowledgement from others, so it's vital that it comes from within and with no expectation for anything from others.

Weeks later, as the merger was coming to a close, I received a call from my old college buddy Kunal Bahl, the one I'd partnered with on our zany SprayIt toilet-seat cleaner back at Wharton. Kunal had long since left behind our dream of saving the world one toilet seat at a time. He was now the cofounder of India's second largest e-commerce company, Delhi-based Snapdeal. Kunal and his partner Rohit Bansal had raised a lot of money. Indeed, with its past infusions totalling $900 million, SoftBank was their largest investor. Now, however, Snapdeal had hit a critical inflection point. With Flipkart, the sector's e-commerce leader, and Amazon threatening to swoop in and devour the Indian market, rumblings were forming suggesting Snapdeal was in trouble.

'Jason,' Kunal said on the phone, 'I need your help on something.'

9

Nothing Worthwhile Comes Easy

I'D ALWAYS LOOKED forward to calls from Kunal. He's the sort of college buddy you know you'll always stay close with—that friend whom, even after months of being apart, you can pick up with right where you left off. Beyond our shared time and memories at Wharton, we're wired with similar values. I'd always admired his gargantuan sense of vision. So when he and Rohit created one of the country's biggest online shopping platforms, I and many others felt proud of the Indian e-commerce story they were helping pioneer.

Started in 2007, Snapdeal had soared to become one of India's earliest startups to hit a billion-dollar valuation. Kunal and Rohit had rightly been hailed as two of the country's youngest entrepreneur rock stars. At its peak, Snapdeal was valued at $6.5 billion. To call Snapdeal's rise meteoric was an understatement.

But by the time Kunal called in December 2016, the hope that Snapdeal might one day become India's version of Amazon.com had already begun to sour.

For one, there was *already* an Amazon.com—a behemoth helmed by the world's richest man, Jeff Bezos. Bezos's net worth is surpassed only by his hunger for limitless scale and e-commerce dominance. Presumably, that might also include swallowing the Indian market. Indeed, Amazon's entry into the Indian market did push Snapdeal into third place.

Second, while Kunal and Rohit may have sometimes been affectionately referred to as the 'Jack Ma's' of India, the actual Jack Ma, the cofounder and chairman of Alibaba, was another e-commerce king circling the Indian ecosystem. Finally, there was the homegrown e-commerce success story out of Bangalore named Flipkart. With investment giants like Tencent, Microsoft, and eBay keeping their coffers flush with cash, Flipkart's cofounders Sachin Bansal and Binny Bansal had rocketed to the top of India's e-commerce market. Initially, Flipkart was in the number one position with Snapdeal in the second. But then Amazon slingshot around Snapdeal pushing it down to number three.

The high-stakes competition inside the e-commerce space wasn't surprising. Titan investors knew whoever planted the most enduring e-commerce flag in India first could potentially rule the sector for decades. Why? Because achieving that sort of Amazon-esque scale is so expensive that once you've captured the market, the barriers to entry become too high and complex for would-be rivals to surmount. As a result, the leader becomes largely cocooned off from competition.

The fact that Amazon's investors had stuck with them through years of unprofitability had taught e-commerce investors to play the long game; those with a long-term vision who were willing to stick it out could come up the big winner. They were willing to go all in and scale at light speed. So no, India's heavyweight e-commerce battle wasn't surprising.

What was eye-opening, however, was the warp-speed manner in which Snapdeal's standing had begun to fall.

Due to the nature of what I do, I seldom receive calls for help when things are going superb. I'd read the business articles enough to know that things at Snapdeal weren't good. But I detected something in Kunal's voice that concerned me even more—a sense that the Snapdeal team wasn't sure of its core strategy versus their competition. And of course it was that very thing—a clear strategy to regain market share and a path to profitability—that Snapdeal's top investors like SoftBank and Nexus Venture Partners all needed to feel confident about, in order to continue giving the company the time and capital it needed to battle Flipkart, Amazon, and others.

'Kunal, I want to help,' I said. 'It sounds like you guys are at a real fork-in-the-road moment. But I have to finish what I started here at Housing.com. We have this complicated merger; I have a responsibility to the company's employees and investors. I need to see it through to completion. It should be a couple of months, probably by January.' That would be the January of 2017.

'Sounds good,' he said. 'When you're done there in Mumbai, let's get you to Delhi so you, Rohit, and I can sit down and discuss this.'

Leaving my post as Housing.com's CEO was emotional for me. My colleagues had become like family. We'd battled through many challenges together, including painful restructurings. We'd created a best-in-class strategy, business model, and operating plan together. And, in the end, this produced a 400 per cent increase in revenues, created the leading platform for buying and selling homes in the country, saved 1,000 jobs, and put the company in News Corp and PropTiger's safe hands. But now, it was time to tell the employees I loved and respected goodbye.

I remember the last time I gathered the hundreds of call centre employees to announce the merger and my resignation. I did my best not to let my voice crack or quaver. After my remarks, a call centre employee took the microphone.

'*Hum badi muskhil mein thhé. Lekin aapki mehnat ki wajah se yaha bahot log apni job rakhne mein kamyab huye hai. Aur ab, humari company ke pass ek ujjaval bhavishya ke liye ek aur mauka hai. Aap humare Dhoni ho*!' he concluded, as the room clapped. [Translation: We were in the dumps. Thanks to your efforts, many of us have managed to keep our jobs. And now, our company has a chance for a brighter future. You are our Dhoni!]. Even as I type those words, I remember feeling so humbled, so grateful for the privilege to lead such dedicated and incredible people. I felt that way then. I feel that way now.

In the eighteen months I served as Housing.com CEO, like all executives, I was forced to make many difficult decisions. In my heart of hearts, I know what I did was right. I did my best to save as many jobs as I could and strengthen the company. But I feel pain, too. And I would be lying if I said I didn't. Some executives say a CEO should never get emotionally invested in one's workforce; better to compartmentalize the natural course of corporate decision-making. Maybe so. That's just not me. Some like to say, *It isn't personal, it's business*. I think that's just some people's way of pretending one can bifurcate what is inextricably bound.

As sad as I was to leave Housing.com, I looked forward to learning how I might help change Snapdeal's future. I'd known some of Snapdeal's largest investors, such as SoftBank and Nexus, for some time now and had forged mutual bonds of respect and trust. The investors made it clear they wanted me to join Snapdeal given all they had at stake. So, as promised, I met with Kunal and Rohit to discuss Snapdeal's problems and to gain a clearer picture of how I could help.

By January 2017 the company's valuation had plunged to a fraction of its previous height of $6.5 billion. What had started as a coupon company had grown into a B2C (business to customer) e-commerce marketplace that sold everything from roti makers to cricket bats. As a result, highly complex decisions about things like logistics (shipping) and online payment systems had been made midstream, without a clear strategy in place to lead the way. The result was not unlike Housing.com when I first joined: a sprawling mishmash of ideas, features, and businesses all in search of a cohesive strategy. Listening to them talk gave me the gnawing feeling that things might be worse under the hood than they appeared on the surface.

Kunal and Rohit are exceedingly bright. There was no question they possessed the talent and ability to right the Snapdeal ship. But the company's explosive growth coincided with an industry boom period that created an environment of over-optimism, excess, and little oversight, often resulting in some faulty long-term decisions.

'We want to be the Alibaba of India,' they explained. 'But Amazon and Flipkart are ahead of us right now, and our investors are beginning to question whether they want to continue pumping capital into us, merge us with Flipkart or someone else, or close shop.'

'I think we should first focus on surviving and then use this chance to create a solid business based on strong fundamentals, one we truly believe in, not a business based on current market or investor perceptions,' I responded.

Kunal and Rohit were adamant that Snapdeal not be sold or merged. This was their baby. They had built an impressive e-commerce platform from scratch. Because I was already part of the SoftBank family through my tenure as Housing.com CEO and had also been an advisor to them, I believed my familiarity with their investors' thinking and expectations might be of help. But more than that, I knew my holistic understanding of how all the pieces of business must come together under an overarching plan could add the most value.

'We'd like to have you join us, Jason,' said Kunal. 'I'm not sure what it would look like exactly, but we need someone we trust who has your kind of experience to provide a new perspective and capabilities during this critical time.'

The opportunity would be the first time I would not be in the CEO role. I'd grown accustomed to having strategic and operating control over decision-making and execution. I knew this job would be all grunt work with no executive sparkle. Still, the idea of serving as the consigliere, strategist, and, I suspected, dealmaker had some appeal, as Kunal was already talented at investor management and marketing, while Rohit was a strong and focused operating leader. Also, being afforded the bandwidth to focus solely on these high value aspects could also potentially lead to making a large impact. More importantly, though, even though I had quite a few CEO offers at this point, I wanted to be there for my close friend when he needed me the most.

But I had two conditions.

'If I join you, I will not be the CEO for the first time in my career. So to make the impact we all hope I will make, I would need to join as a partner to you and Rohit and be involved in all major decision-making; also, I would want to bring some of my top guys from Housing.com with me,' I said.

'Of course, we know that and have the same thing in mind. For example, even in meetings with investors, like Masa, we would want you to be there. On the second point, we usually have a process for new hires,' Kunal replied.

'I respect that. But I vouch for them. They were at my side and you see the results we got at Housing.com. Besides, you don't have the luxury of a long-drawn-out hiring process. They were loyal to me and I'm loyal to them. Their names are Dilip Tuli, Abhishek Hota, and Darpan Khurana. They know how I think, what I expect, and are top talents. That will save time and add tremendous value to the company. So I would need them to come with me.'

Kunal and Rohit were agreeable. My official title at Snapdeal would be chief strategy and investment officer. So, in January 2017, I packed up my Mumbai apartment and relocated to Delhi so I could get to work as quickly as possible.

On my very first day on the job, they hit me with the news.

'Due to our cash crunch,' said Rohit, 'we may have to lay off 90 per cent of our 4,000 employees.'

He might as well have punched me in the windpipe.

Dear God, I thought, *this seriously can't be happening all over again. Not another mass layoff horror show!*

Given Rohit's witty sense of humour, I thought maybe he was just pulling a prank on me.

'Rohit, you're joking, right? Please tell me you're kidding me,' I said.

'Totally serious.'

'Well, let me tell you something right now. You can't cut 90 per cent of Snapdeal's workforce.'

'Why?'

'Because the attrition will kill the remaining 10 per cent. And then you'll have nothing.'

He paused and thought.

I continued: 'What's most important right now is that we cannot have knee-jerk decision-making. All the zigging and zagging all over the place is part of why the company is in the predicament it's in.'

Kunal chimed in.

'Well, this cash crunch has accelerated things considerably. So do you think you could come up with the solution in, like, two weeks?'

'Two weeks?' I howled. 'Two weeks! Guys, you couldn't come up with a solution in ten *years*! And now you're seriously thinking I'm going to walk in here and cook up a solution that fast?'

We all shared a nervous chuckle.

'Look, time and money are not on our side right now. I get it. But our greatest threat is poor strategic planning and execution. You guys are too close, too enmeshed in the business that you're not able to pull back. I want to help make decisions based on data and hard facts. My team and I are going to move as quickly and efficiently as possible. But this has to be done right.'

They nodded.

'Now tell me … how much cash do we really have?' I asked.

'About three to six months,' said Kunal.

Given those hard financial realities, it was determined in late February 2017 that 1,000 people would need to be laid off immediately. Since I was the one with restructuring experience, I would be the one managing the painful process, including meeting with each C-level employee, breaking the news to them, and creating and managing their restructuring plan with them.

This would also help insulate Kunal and Rohit from the natural ill-will that mass layoffs create with the management team. I knew I was about to become extremely unpopular, but it was the right thing to do for the company.

In Kunal's email to employees, he explained the reason for the painful decision:

> We started growing our business much before the right economic model and market fit was figured out. We also started diversifying and starting new projects while we still hadn't perfected the first or made it profitable. We started building our team and capabilities for a much larger size of business than what was required with the present scale.

He vowed that he and Rohit would work with no pay.

> Both Rohit and I are taking a 100 per cent salary cut. Many of our leaders have also stepped up proactively and offered to take a significant cut in their compensation.

Finally, he explained the road that lay ahead:

> We are combining teams, reducing layers, eliminating non-core projects and strengthening the focus on profitable growth. Sadly, we will also be saying really painful goodbyes to some of our colleagues in this process. This is, by far, the hardest decision we have ever taken.

Unfortunately, this was not the first round of Snapdeal layoffs, nor would it be the last on the way to trying to rescue the company. Whether SoftBank and the other investors would wait that long before selling Snapdeal to Flipkart, some other company, or shut down the company altogether was the question that hovered ominously over us as we sped towards a solution.

I knew what I wanted. My core team and I were going to create a fully baked plan. I didn't want any subjective fluff marring our strategy.

Just sharp, clear, data-driven solutions. My vision was a plan that was so rigorously and exhaustively researched that it would be devoid of lazy logic or emotionalism. We were going to grind nonstop. Wake up … research from morning until morning … steal a few hours of sleep … and then get up and do it all over again. I would have a zero-tolerance policy for suggestions based on hocus-pocus hopes and wishes. Instead, we were going to keep our heads out of the sky and our hands in the soil.

Because I wasn't serving as the company's leader, I didn't need to devote as much time and energy to meeting many of the company's thousands of employees. Nevertheless, I wanted to learn as much as possible from those who had been with the company the longest. I then settled in with my team of Dilip, Abhishek, and Darpan to create a 'war-room' level of intensity and focus on the task ahead. Joining us was Rathin Rawal, a skilled Snapdeal talent who was already with the company when we arrived.

'For the next three months, we are going to embark on the most exhaustive and comprehensive deep research that has ever been done in the Indian e-commerce space,' I told my team. 'You can and should expect to work into the early morning hours. Snapdeal is in a fight for survival. There's no time to waste. This will likely be some of the most important work you do in your careers. This work may be the difference between remaining an independent company or being sold or shut down, which would wipe out billions of dollars of value and thousands of jobs. We don't want that to happen. That means we are going to work harder than ever to find a winning business model that will add years of runway in front of our company.'

The top-secret Snapdeal 2.0 plan we were about to embark upon became known internally by the codename 'Project Argonaut'. It was a historical allusion to the Greek myth of 'Jason and the Argonauts'—a story about a young leader and his crew of heroes, including Hercules, known as the Argonauts, who went on a seemingly insurmountable and dangerous quest aboard the ship *Argo* in search of the Golden Fleece. I hoped our journey would prove equally as rewarding.

Creating the Snapdeal 2.0 plan involved deep dives into countries and markets, detailed financial analyses, and complex synthesizing of large amounts of data and information to clearly understand the evolution of companies, including the specific context and causal factors behind successes or failures in each case. But in its simplest form, we had three driving goals.

First, we would study key e-commerce markets and players globally to draw learnings for the Indian market. Next, we would identify a specific business model for India market dominance or successful coexistence with other well-funded e-commerce players. Finally, we would define Snapdeal's new business strategy and an operational plan to establish a clear path forward to building a large, profitable, and valuable company.

To begin, I first directed my team to identify and study every major e-commerce company in the world. China's Alibaba, Taobao.com and JD.com, America's Amazon and eBay, Latin America's Mercado Libre and B2W Digital, Southeast Asia's Tokopedia and Lazada, Japan's Rakuten and Yahoo! Japan, the Middle East's Souq—we spanned the globe in search of e-commerce players covering diverse geographies and business models.

From there, we then dissected each e-commerce company's core model and financials. As you might imagine, there was quite a mix. Some were B2C platforms, such as Amazon, Lazada, and JD.com. In these arrangements, the business amassed a large inventory of products from vendors and stocked their warehouses with goods to be shipped to paying customers. Within the B2C platform, there were also managed marketplaces where merchants could list products and then the e-commerce platform would fulfil orders and handle the nuts and bolts, like logistics and packaging.

The advantages of the B2C model were that you could provide the best user experience, higher commission rates, visibility into stock levels, and faster delivery with better brand credibility. But there were negatives too. You had to have massive capital to warehouse an enormous inventory of products, resulting in questionable profitability and a longer time to achieve scale.

Then there were the C2C or pure marketplace e-commerce players, like Taobao.com. In this set-up, the business would serve as a platform where individuals or small mom-and-pop retailers, not just large sellers, could sell their goods directly to customers. Within this model there were several variants. For example, some focused solely on new product sales. Others, like eBay, offered a hybrid of new and used goods. And then others, such as India's Quikr, focused on creating a niche for used good sales. Most of these required the seller to handle shipping the products.

The advantages of the pure marketplace model were that it was highly scalable with a high capital efficiency and profitability. Why? Because you had no warehouse or logistics to hassle with. This meant you could have the largest selection and low prices due to having so many sellers, all competing with one another. The downside was that many users reported lacklustre user experiences. Others expressed reticence trusting small and unknown sellers who might or might not provide quality customer service for things like returns or damaged products.

With the players and models now on the Snapdeal 2.0 whiteboard, it was time to study whether each model coexisted with others in each market. The key takeaways were revealing. B2C and pure marketplace business models successfully coexisted with each other in all markets. You had Amazon (B2C) coexisting alongside eBay (pure marketplace). Or Japan's Rakuten (B2C) and Amazon Japan (B2C) coexisting beside Yahoo! Japan (pure marketplace).

But there were additional insights to be gleaned from these cross-model comparisons. For example, no more than two B2C players had ever succeeded long term in any market. Also, outside of Amazon in the US, no other inventory-based model had achieved meaningful profitability in any market globally. As for the pure marketplace models, they had demonstrated high scalability and profitability in all markets.

Best of all, we discovered that the more unorganized the retail market was in a region, the higher the odds that the pure marketplace model would succeed. And it was this last point that blipped my and my team's strategic radar.

Why were pure marketplace models better suited to looser, less-organized markets like India, as opposed to highly structured ecosystems like the United States? It turns out there are several reasons. For one, pure marketplace models are better suited for local sellers which India is replete with (think *kirana* stores).

Having access to an e-commerce marketplace allows small mom-and-pop sellers to capture a higher share of total sales, simplifies the mind-numbingly complex world of online selling, and doesn't compete with sellers the way the inventory model does. The pure marketplace model also gives consumers a wider selection of products to choose from and lower prices driven by stiff competition.

Perhaps best of all, allowing smaller sellers to get online and sell their products directly allows the marketplace to be better suited to serve local customer preferences. No one knows what local people want to buy better than local sellers, who understand and are a part of the same culture. And it was this key emphasis on local and cultural buyer preferences that would continue to push our Snapdeal 2.0 team sailing towards the pure marketplace model, as we burned the midnight oil and dined on takeout food until two or three o'clock many mornings.

With a firm grasp around the global landscape, the models, and the interactions between them, it was now time to laser in on India. Our retail market is dominated by small, traditional retailers. In fact, at the time, 90 per cent of our retail market was comprised of so-called 'unorganized' local sellers. That means we have among the lowest share of organized retail in the world. Also, we currently have limited retail space relative to the large population size compared to developed countries.

In other words, India represents a massive entrepreneurial opportunity with huge headroom for growth. We have very few large-scale brick-and-mortar retailers. Sure, we have retailers like D-Mart, Big Bazaar, and More. But when you compare their size to, say, Walmart, Target, or TJX Companies in the US, they are fractional. Put simply, what this means is that Indian retailers have low bargaining power with suppliers leading to one of the lowest gross margins globally.

On the flip side, our *kirana* stores do exceptionally well on cost structure. Lower labour costs, lower maintenance costs, and lower rent or real estate costs (some even operating out of a home or residence), all result in better profitability than organized players. Bottom line: our small merchants will continue to thrive in India due to their structural advantages.

Now why does that matter? It matters because if you know that small sellers are hardwired into the Indian market, and that the pure marketplace e-commerce platform can empower and grow those little mom-and-pops by getting their goods online to reach a massive audience, you can capture a big slice of India's enormous online shopping landscape.

In 2016, online shopping in India was a $13 billion market. But by 2025, our analyses determined Indian e-commerce would be a

$200 billion opportunity. Now, you might look at the gulf between those numbers—$13 billion and $200 billion—and wonder how in the world such growth is possible in the span of just nine years. To that I would ask you this question: how quickly did the life of everyone you know change when your friends, parents, and Aunty started using WhatsApp? Overnight there was an explosion of game-changing technology that transformed the way people all across our country communicate and interact. The same will be true for online shopping.

Consider this. Roughly half of our population is between fifteen and forty-five years of age. 'Young India' will be among the fastest adopters of e-commerce buying habits. We're also rapidly strengthening the quality and reach of our internet connectivity, digital payment systems, and affordable access to smartphones and tablets, and are seeing the emergence of strong third-party-logistics service providers (the people who handle all the shipping and delivery of packages—more on that in a bit).

What will all these younger, rising, connected Indians want to buy online? Well, Dilip, Abhishek, Darpan, Rathin, and I studied that, too. Interestingly, when you look at new goods versus used goods, you realize that the lion's share of the future market will belong to new goods. This is particularly true among Indians. Our consumers believe in high value extraction, which means we use our products longer than other cultures. For example, the average laptop lifetime in India is roughly five years, whereas globally the number is three years. Our buying behaviours also skew towards trust and avoiding risk. When you buy a used product that's broken or defective, it often lacks a warranty or service agreement to replace it. These quality verification challenges are difficult to overcome in an online environment where buyers are wary of getting ripped off.

So if you know that Indians are going to be buying more new stuff, that smaller, more local retailers are inherently positioned to succeed in the ecosystem, and that a pure marketplace e-commerce platform can coexist successfully regardless of whether the giants of global e-commerce come tromping into the market, what's the smartest move?

Although the pure marketplace environment was in a nascent stage at the time of our analysis, it was projected to become as large as the B2C market by 2025. Grabbing a big chunk of that would hinge on understanding what sellers of all sizes needed and wanted. So we conducted a seller analysis. Seller surveys showed they wanted an easy way to list their products online and a simplified payment process that made sure payments were on time with no hidden charges or fees.

The results of all our research were clear and undeniable—pure marketplace. Indian e-commerce was a large and untapped opportunity that was ripe for disruption. The pure marketplace business model mitigated the threat of global entrants because it required a localized and customized approach that produced strong network effects (*every* dominant pure marketplace company in the world was a local player). In the coming years, global players would struggle to build a pure marketplace e-commerce play in India in the same way that Amazon struggled (and ultimately failed) to take over China, where homegrown Alibaba had zoomed ahead.

Deciphering whether and how Snapdeal could achieve such a feat was the Snapdeal 2.0 team's next task.

It's important to appreciate just how complex large-scale e-commerce really is. Back when I was a kid in Agra bartering on the street with that annoyed chessboard vendor, the transaction was as simple as it gets. There was a seller (him), a buyer (me), money (₹30), and a product (the chessboard). I gave him money; he gave me a chessboard. End of story.

But when buying and selling happens online at scale, hundreds of variables instantly crowd the transactional landscape. Customer website and app development, seller website and app development, seller acquisition, seller on-boarding, supply chain management, warehousing, logistics, reverse logistics (returns), digital payments (including integration with multiple wallets, banks, card networks), customer service, server/cloud storage, data security, advertisement conversion rates, customer ratings, seller ratings and feedback, fraud detection systems … the dizzying list goes on and on.

Put it this way: there's a reason it took Amazon so long to turn a profit. Mass e-commerce isn't a business for beginners. But that's also why it represents such a massive opportunity. Because if you can somehow make sense of it all, untangle the insanity, and then create an easy-to-use seller platform for *other* people that handles all the headaches … well, then you're positioned to potentially make billions.

The two biggest hassles e-commerce companies have to solve are how to accept electronic payments and how to handle logistics.

Snapdeal had addressed these issues before I joined, by acquiring two companies to handle each. In 2015, Snapdeal had paid $400 million (largely using Snapdeal stock as consideration near its peak valuation) for a company called FreeCharge—one of India's largest digital payment companies. On paper, it was the largest acquisition in India of an internet company. The idea was that maybe one day it could become like Alipay for Alibaba. But as you'll see, that didn't happen.

For end-to-end logistics and supply chain solutions, Snapdeal had purchased and further invested in a company named Vulcan

Express with approximately 4,000 employees. These employees had the job of handling everything from packing the products, routing the deliveries of all customer packages, physically managing the delivery of those orders, providing digital tracking to ensure proper fulfilment, and handling things like returned packages or damage replacement.

Originally, Snapdeal had made the decision to buy FreeCharge and Vulcan Express because it was striving to be a B2C e-commerce giant. And in that scenario, just like Amazon.com or Alibaba, it would need to warehouse massive inventory and process millions of digital payment transactions. So, instead of outsourcing those tasks to third-party digital transaction or logistics companies, Snapdeal acquired businesses to do it for them.

Initially, we thought there may be an opportunity to unlock potential synergies between Snapdeal and FreeCharge. We observed that there were massive synergies globally between digital payment businesses and e-commerce platforms. For people in America, if they shopped on eBay, the vast majority (75 per cent) paid for their purchases using PayPal. In China, 50 per cent of all Alibaba transactions were completed using Alipay. Likewise, Latin American customers on Mercado Libre disproportionately used Mercado Pago to buy things. Could we create a similar digital payment synergy between Snapdeal and FreeCharge by making it the default payment option? At first, we were hopeful that might be possible.

But one thing we knew right away was that Vulcan Express had to go. In fact, it was more dire than that. If we didn't unload the logistics company, our calculations and projections showed, it would be the anchor that sunk Snapdeal. The service itself was solid. The problem was the numbers; they didn't add up or make any sense. It destroyed the company's unit economics or profitability. We needed to sell it. Fast.

The savings from unloading the company's costs also might, we hoped, buy us some time and keep our investors from selling us to Flipkart. In its place, we would transition to using third-party logistics companies that could be integrated into our platform. Besides, if we were going to move Snapdeal from a B2C business to a pure marketplace company, product fulfilment would now be the sole responsibility of the seller, with Snapdeal acting as a facilitator. Just think of the cost savings that no longer tackling massive warehouse inventory management would generate. Then multiply that times all the boxes, packaging tracking, delivery, returns, damaged product replacement, etc.

Kunal, Rohit, and I agreed that I and my team would come up with a Snapdeal 2.0 plan, which would create a sustainable, profitable, and valuable business model for Snapdeal. This, in turn, would convince the board and investors that we knew what we were doing and demonstrate that Snapdeal should not be sold. I believed that was exactly what me and my team had devised.

'Well, gang,' I told my team, 'it's time to build the most impressive slide presentation we've ever created. We need to work extremely hard to distil the core strategy down for the founders and board. I want our presentation to be irrefutable, which means completely based on data and logic. It also should be easy to understand and self-explanatory as a document, so that it flows like a story with crystal-clear conclusions. It better not be a data dump or open to any interpretation.'

My eyes scanned the room, bouncing from Darpan to Rathin to Dilip before finally stopping on Abhishek.

'We're only going to get one shot at this. I fully expect pushback and resistance, especially from the founders and anyone instrumental in building the company in its current state, because accepting changes that undo some of your efforts and work is always difficult. So let's work extra hard to craft our presentation in such a way that it anticipates and addresses their questions and concerns before they even express them.'

The founders and board would either recognize the Snapdeal 2.0 plan's value or resist and kill its tough love conclusions. We were about to find out which.

10

Not Every Seed Is Meant to Bloom a Forest

I WOKE UP extra early. This was the day I would submit the Snapdeal 2.0 plan to two groups: the founders and the board.

Everything needed to be crisp and perfect. I sat on my bed, bathed in the glow of my laptop. Over and over I scanned each of the 100 slides hunting for typos, spacing blunders, or transposed digits. I refused to allow errors which could cause the founders or the board to dismiss our plan to save the company.

As I reviewed the presentation, I thought back to two meetings I'd had several months earlier involving Masa. One of these took place at the rooftop restaurant at the Leela Palace hotel in Chankayapuri,

Delhi. Masa had been in town for a day but was tied up meeting with the prime minister. He finally arrived around dinner time for a series of meetings.

The meeting was casual. Masa and Kunal were at one table and I and a few others at another. Snapdeal needed money bad. If Masa was in a deal-making mode, the goal was for Kunal to pin him down on a deal to shore up Snapdeal's cash burn.

That night Masa was his usual polite and jubilant self. His manners are soft and gracious. But make no mistake, entrepreneurs do not come more competitive than him. Masa had seen how Jack Ma had carved out Alipay, which went on to become a $150 billion online and mobile payment platform. Alipay's success had stirred Masa's competitive juices; he was keen on advancing into the digital payments space. So much so, he was interested in buying FreeCharge from Snapdeal.

Here's how fast Masa took action. He grabbed a napkin and scribbled out a possible deal. Ultimately, that deal didn't come to fruition. But that's how quick SoftBank could move. I knew that if our Snapdeal 2.0 plan was ill-received, and we were unable to gain buy-in from the board to implement it, that's exactly how fast SoftBank might sell us to Flipkart.

I then reflected on a different Masa meeting that had taken place during my transition from Housing.com to Snapdeal. That meeting was held around a sleek mahogany boardroom table at the Leela. SoftBank president Alok Sama arrived dressed in a suit. That was a bit unusual, he typically dressed more casual (think Steve Jobs).

Seated around the table were a handful of their Indian CEOs and founders, which now included companies like Hike, Grofers, Inmobi, Oyo, Ola, and Snapdeal, among others. Masa was flying his private jet from Saudi Arabia and was running late. When he arrived, he apologized for his tardiness before launching into an exuberant discussion about a historic moment in business. In fact, he was so excited he couldn't sit. The news? Masa said he was going to create the largest-ever fund in business history, something that would later become known as the Vision Fund.

'I'm so excited!' he said. 'We're raising the largest fund ever in history—$100 billion!' He explained that he had just been with MBS (Mohammad bin Salman), the Crown Prince of Saudi Arabia. In a forty-five minute pitch, he'd secured $45 billion.

'What do you think about that?' Masa exclaimed. We were astonished. Masa then explained that he wanted to raise a $100 billion fund every few years, because he planned to deploy the cash fast. The whole thing seemed unbelievable; we thought he was exaggerating, as this would be by far the largest fund ever created.

He'd also apparently had a phone call on the way from the airport from the founder of Ola, Bhavish Aggarwal, who now sat with us in the room.

'And on my way from the airport, Bhavish and I were discussing doing a deal involving one million electric cars! So exciting!' Masa said as Bhavish smiled at him.

Good grief ... why can't I be Bhavish?, I thought.

Masa's animated delivery made it next to impossible not to smile. People like to joke that there's very little that doesn't excite Masa. His passion for deal-making and entrepreneurship are infectious. And when it comes to a grand vision, few can hold a candle to him. So it should have come as no surprise when he later pulled off his historic $100 billion Vision Fund.

Masa's mind is always future-focused. He's a believer in what's known as 'the singularity', the belief that the convergence of technology and human biology will create a world only seen in sci-fi movies, one where technological growth and artificial intelligence (AI) hit an inflection point that triggers seismic, irreversible alterations to human existence. How far does he think it will go? Well, Masa has even presented on telepathy (which seemed to me an eerie coincidence to the Harbinger character Harada). Bottom line: Masa's vision is one of the rarest in the world.

When he finally got down to the business at hand, Masa made his expectations crystal clear.

'You are part of this Softbank family,' he said. 'If you're a winner in your space, there will be unlimited money for you. But if you're not, I will have no money for you.' His directness let every CEO in the room know that he meant what he said. He added, 'I have a track record of 44 per cent IRR [internal rate of return or annualized return], so don't hurt my return! I will only invest if this expected return is met or exceeded!'

No pressure.

With those two realities floating in my mind—that investor decisions can happen with blinding, back-of-a-napkin speed, and that performance would seal the fate of future funding—I submitted the Snapdeal 2.0 plan to the founders and the board.

Then, we waited.

The founders were on board almost immediately. 'It's clear a ton of work went into this,' said Kunal.

'And we think you're right,' said Rohit. 'This is the framework for a solution.'

I was floored. All along I'd prepared myself for a courtroom-style shootout complete with hard-hitting cross-examinations. I never anticipated that they'd be persuaded so quickly. But their decisiveness and willingness to take action was a testament to their maturity as leaders.

The instant they saw the collective efforts of my team's three-month Snapdeal 2.0 initiative, they knew the plan could help them achieve the independence Snapdeal desired. Just because they agreed with the plan, however, didn't mean accepting its conclusions had been easy. But like all smart executives, they understood that desperate corporate times call for deft and daring strategic measures.

As for the board, its members asked some small follow-up questions, which my team and I satisfactorily addressed. The board then approved the Snapdeal 2.0 plan. The real challenge was that Snapdeal's main investor—Softbank—wasn't willing to provide the additional funding to implement that 2.0 plan. They liked the plan, but they had lost confidence in the company. They had already worked out a merger with Flipkart and were pushing hard to make it happen. So, with no money to execute the Snapdeal 2.0 plan, and with Softbank speeding towards a Flipkart merger, we had to do something big and bold to create another path or at least buy us some time.

The first thing we did was to devise an alternative merger proposal with a different company that had clear synergies. This would not be a bluff, but instead a real merger deal. We knew gaining board approval would be a long shot, but if we could present a billion-dollar merger plan end-to-end—complete with a term sheet—the emergence of a new opportunity might make the Snapdeal board pause, evaluate it carefully, and if not approved, at worst, give us the block of time we needed to somehow generate the cash we needed to implement our Snapdeal 2.0 plan instead of being sold.

And that's exactly what happened. I managed to negotiate a different merger plan with another company in three weeks. This company had clear synergies—complementary businesses, access to a new set of investors, and like-minded founders whom we had great chemistry with. The Snapdeal board was surprised and pleased to see a serious second merger possibility materialize so quickly. There were now three paths on the table: a Snapdeal-Flipkart merger; the alternative Snapdeal merger deal; implementing the Snapdeal 2.0 plan my team and I had created.

The founders and I wanted to move forward with the third option of implementing the Snapdeal 2.0 plan. The board passed on the second option of an alternative merger deal and wanted to pursue the Flipkart merger. I and our attorneys then helped the founders realize how their legal rights could be used to reject and block that from happening, which would allow us to go forward on implementing the Snapdeal 2.0 plan.

Founders should understand that they really wear at least three hats that, depending on the forum they are in, require different thinking and action. As a board member, you have a fiduciary responsibility to act in the best interest of the shareholders and vote in favour of options that maximize value creation. As a CEO, you have to do what the board approves and instructs. And as a shareholder, you have no obligation to anyone and can do as you please.

Therefore, depending on your rights in the shareholder agreement, you can vote whichever way you like with no justification to anyone. Based on their shareholder rights, this is what Kunal and Rohit eventually did. Snapdeal's two largest investors—Softbank and Nexus—then conceded and agreed to go ahead with implementing Snapdeal 2.0, resulting in board majority approval of executing our plan. The strategy presented a clear justification of greater shareholder value creation, including financial projections and valuation. Even though some non-board member shareholders aggressively disagreed, the board's decision was the final say.

We had successfully staved off the immediate merger with Flipkart and gained board approval to execute the Snapdeal 2.0 strategy. How long we could keep the merger chatter at bay we weren't sure. After all, we were still in desperate need of cash to fully implement our plan. But for the time being, we were at least greenlit to give it a shot and battle to execute the Snapdeal 2.0 plan.

We needed to move quickly. The cash crunch was dire. In fact, consolidated losses at the time were over $20 million a month.

Snapdeal had once been a rock star of the e-commerce space. Now it was stuck between a rock and a hard place and had been forced to switch to survival mode.

I knew the gravity of it all weighed heavy on Kunal and Rohit. On a plane ride around this time Kunal shared his concerns. 'This feels like a nightmare. I can't believe this has happened. I just can't believe it.' To see my old college buddy going through this hurt me. But more than anything, it redoubled my commitment to help him battle through it. 'You're not a complete leader without this,' I said trying to reassure him. 'You will become a much stronger leader and businessman for all of this.' I believed the words I was speaking. Still, having myself worn the executive crown in my previous posts, I knew no amount of cheerleading could lift a besieged CEO's spirits.

Snapdeal's treatment in the Indian press wasn't helping either. Rivals smelling blood in the water were happy to pile on, to spark a media feeding frenzy. In 2016, the company had roughly 9,000 employees. By the time I arrived in 2017 and after the February round of layoffs, that number was just under 1,900. And there was more consolidation still ahead. To say the headlines and reports were bruising would be to put it mildly.

The only thing that could dig Snapdeal out of this hole was old-fashioned performance and results. We needed to begin the migration from a B2C business towards a pure marketplace business in an effort to turn Snapdeal's massive monthly losses into an operating profit. The restructuring goals included achieving an optimal organization structure and cost base to execute on the new business model and strategy, and extending the company's runway by reducing the funding requirement to break even.

To have any chance of achieving these overarching goals, Snapdeal would need to undergo the same kind of gut-grinding restructuring we had been forced to implement earlier. With all the stress of the moment, there were times when Kunal and I clashed. But the reason our friendship lasted through it all was because we shared similar values. I knew Kunal well enough to know this was as painful for him as Housing.com's layoffs were for me. But there was no other way to save the company.

Just as we were about to begin these layoffs, Kunal and Rohit got rattled. It seemed someone had written and circulated a scorching letter to the media and others trashing them. From the tone of their voices and the pained expressions on their faces, they were clearly upset by the unfair accusations and attacks.

'We can't do these layoffs,' they told me.

'But it's the right thing to do,' I said. 'We can't save the remaining employees' jobs and build a profitable company without the cuts.'

They stared at me stoically.

'Here,' I said, 'hand me the letter so I can look at it.'

The first thing I noticed was that it was written in an unsophisticated manner; it was more of a rant, less a serious argument. The second thing that caught my eye was the bottom of the note, there was no signature or name attached.

'Guys, this is an anonymous letter,' I said. 'What they're saying about you isn't true. Relax. Take a breath. Step back and look at the bigger business picture here. This isn't going to be easy. But it's the only way.'

They knew it was the right thing to do for the company. But that didn't make it any easier. I empathized completely. Perhaps the fact that I was not as emotionally connected to Snapdeal in the same way I had been at Housing.com and Valiant made it slightly less difficult for me to press forward. As the strategist and counsellor, I knew I would absorb a big portion of the blame and be disliked. At one point I had to get private security again. Next door at Maruti, a human resources executive had been burned to death and ninety-one employees arrested during a similar exercise. It was an anxious time.

Beyond the looming round of additional job cuts, there was also the issue of dealing with two of the biggest companies that Snapdeal owned—FreeCharge and Vulcan Express.

Around midnight, I went home after a long day at the Snapdeal offices and was walking into the lobby of my apartment building when the phone rang. It was Kunal.

'Hey, what's up?' I answered.

'Govind Rajan just resigned.' Govind Rajan was the CEO of FreeCharge.

'Wait, what?'

'He's out.'

'Oh … wow … ok.'

'Are you interested?'

'In what?'

'In the CEO position for FreeCharge.'

'Well, um … whatever is best for our cause. But let me think about it a bit.'

'There's no time. The employees and media are already emailing and calling. I need to get back to them right away.'

I paused and stayed silent.

'Jason, you there?'

'Yes … yes.'

'Well? What do you think?'

'Okay,' I said, 'I'll do it.'

A CEO in 60 seconds. That's what I'd just become.

Specifically, I was the CEO of a digital wallet company that had previously been bought for $400 million but had since fallen off the valuation cliff.

The CEO appointment to FreeCharge happened so fast I didn't have time to process it. It was a position most people would kill for. But I was a newcomer to the digital payment business and the fintech sector more broadly. Snapdeal was in a serious bind. They needed an experienced business leader they could trust. A person with the right risk tolerance to jump in, without needing to be coached up on the back story to gain institutional knowledge.

If no one had taken the CEO job right away, top talent inside the company would see the warning signs and begin abandoning ship, which would create a potentially fatal downward spiral for the asset. Also, given the thrashing Snapdeal was already suffering in the press, that would create yet another crisis the company could not afford.

So, from March to October 2017, while still helping implement the Snapdeal 2.0 plan, I served as FreeCharge's CEO.

In the beginning, I was excited about entering the fascinating world of digital payments. I approached the CEO role with the hope of finding a possible solution for how FreeCharge might fit in within the Snapdeal 2.0 vision and plan.

I pulled my inner circle together to conduct a miniature version of our Snapdeal 2.0 study for FreeCharge (FreeCharge 2.0). And that's when I had to confront the harshest of realities—Snapdeal's survival hinged on us divesting of FreeCharge as quickly as possible. No matter how much I may have wanted to serve as the company's CEO to help turn it around, my first duty was helping the founders achieve the goal of saving Snapdeal.

The instant our team pulled together its research I knew my objective must be to begin guiding the company towards a sale. For one, FreeCharge was doing things to boost their scale but not to increase their value long term. They had a great product in terms of user experience, but they hadn't thought through their business. The business plan I inherited said the company required a mind-boggling $700 million and seven years just to break even. And that was using optimistic assumptions!

Second, our in-depth analyses determined that to make money, an electronic payments company would need to have a massive market share. To be sure, the sector was going to be huge, but the digital wallet business was a commoditized product with a race to the bottom in terms of fees charged to consumers. The field was already extremely crowded with competitors like Paytm, Mobikwik, Google Pay, Whatsapp Pay, Naspers/ PayU, and even the government with BHIM and their open Unified Payments Interface (UPI) architecture.

Third—and perhaps most importantly—the sector was about to get swept up in the surging currents of fast-moving regulatory change. The looming regulatory environment was about to make the business unviable. Simply put, when future regulatory guidelines came out with challenging requirements for companies licensed for pre-paid payment instruments(PPI), it was going to be a bloodbath.

As if all that weren't enough, I had also inherited a Foreign Exchange Management Act (FEMA) issue at FreeCharge. The Reserve Bank of India (RBI) said the original FreeCharge deal was done in an illegal way that related to the round tripping of money. The FreeCharge founders and Snapdeal were accused of wrongdoing.

According to the letter of the law, Snapdeal's violation could expose the company to a fine of up to $1 billion. We resolved this through multiple meetings with RBI wherein we explained our position and paid approximately $2 million and dodged a $1 billion bullet that would, suffice it to say, have crushed not only FreeCharge but Snapdeal as well.

Despite all this, there was yet another reason for Snapdeal to sell FreeCharge, one that was equally pressing—the company desperately needed the cash to implement the restructuring plan and Snapdeal 2.0. We had successfully fended off being sold to Flipkart once before. But we knew merger plans would quickly resume and intensify if we didn't solve the cash crunch. How much money could

Snapdeal make by selling its digital payment company? We didn't know. But one thing was for sure: it would be nowhere near the $400 million Snapdeal had purchased FreeCharge for, back in 2015. Given its atrophied valuation, we'd be lucky to get even 10 per cent of that amount.

Selling FreeCharge to generate quick cash assumed two things. First, that we could find a buyer. And second, that I could convince FreeCharge's employees to stay and not quit the company before or during the sale. Fortunately, I was able to accomplish the latter (more on that in a bit). Pulling off the former fast enough to get the cash to keep Snapdeal afloat, however, was going to take something approaching a minor miracle.

Originally, Deutsche Bank was hired to manage the sale. But I quickly realized that was going to be too slow and a bad fit for our code red situation. So I terminated the arrangement. Our team would run the sale directly. First, we identified twenty-five potential buyers to pitch to. Instead of sending each party an identical portfolio of information about why they should buy FreeCharge, our team went the extra mile and crafted customized sales pitches for each of the potential buyers. This required added work and research. But by understanding each company's unique needs and desires, we were able to include more persuasive deal points and sales triggers designed to ignite interest more quickly.

On the operating side, as soon as I became the CEO I met with all of FreeCharge's employees (approximately 230 people), held a series of interactive discussions, and did my best to get a quick assessment on the health of the business from managers and top talent. I hustled to do relationship-building at a quickened clip through my usual mix of talks and town halls. I needed to recondition the company to think in terms of monetization, sustainable scale, and a path to profitability—not growth at all costs.

In only a couple of months, the company made big strides on these fronts and achieved gross profit positive (inclusive of all marketing and promotions costs) for the first-time in its seven-year history. This was quite a contrast to its gross loss a few months earlier of ₹67 crore!

The two-pronged approach on the divestment strategy and business profitability paid off. Axis Bank became interested. The deal was extremely complex, with many moving pieces to negotiate. For example, Axis wanted to build several metrics into the pricing of the deal—things like attrition, scale, and a host of other variables. We rolled up our sleeves, worked around the clock, configured the complicated pricing formula, and managed to complete the sale in one of the fastest and most well-executed deals Axis Bank said it had ever done.

Amazon tried to swoop in at the last minute with a marginally higher offer, but the Axis deal was more certain; we were convinced this was the best home for FreeCharge, and we had also given Axis our word. In the end, Axis Bank agreed to retain all of FreeCharge's 200+ employees and bought the company from Snapdeal for $60 million in cash. It was a landmark deal—the first bank in India to acquire a fintech company.

'This is a win-win deal that allows Snapdeal to further focus on our core e-commerce business, while giving Axis Bank some of the most agile and innovative capabilities in the financial services space in the country,' Kunal told the media.

Understand this: in business, not every seed is meant to bloom a forest. Sometimes the most important decision an entrepreneur makes is knowing when to pull the plug. You have to understand what a sunk cost is and not throw good money after bad. These decisions are often among the most agonizing an entrepreneur encounters. As battle-hardened business-people, we've conditioned ourselves to never quit, never accept defeat. And that's what's so deceiving about divestments or the closing of business lines or geographies—what on the surface may appear to be a 'loss' may actually be the key that unlocks the door to future strategic wins.

That's exactly what happened in the case of Snapdeal's decision to sell its digital wallet company, FreeCharge. FreeCharge was not relevant to Snapdeal's core business, but it stood to take the company down. Acquisitions that are not thought through are likely to fail. That's what happened here. I can safely say that had we not sold FreeCharge, Snapdeal wouldn't be around today. Why? Because it desperately needed that $60 million to staunch the monthly cash drain and stop it from being sold.

As Kunal later explained, 'The FreeCharge sale was an important part of Snapdeal 2.0 and without that capital, our survival as a company would have been at risk.' Even though news of the FreeCharge sale became public in late July 2017, the transfer of funds didn't happen instantly. 'It took a few visits to RBI to sensitize the decision makers to the gravity of this deal for the survival of the company,' stated Kunal. 'When we finally received the money in October 2017, with not much money left in the bank, I knew that we had turned the corner on our money worries.'

The FreeCharge anchor was no longer weighing down the Snapdeal ship. But there were still dangerous shoals to navigate up ahead. Selling FreeCharge had given us a fresh infusion of $60 million. Still, it was the resource-draining (capital and management bandwidth) vortex of Snapdeal's logistics company—Vulcan Express—that threatened to sink us permanently.

If FreeCharge was a seed not meant to bloom a forest, I was convinced that Vulcan Express was a poison seed that would rot and topple a thousand trees. My conviction on the matter had nothing to do with the logistics company or its employees. They did excellent work. They also benefitted from being led by veteran CEO Hardeep Singh—an executive whose impressive corporate pedigree included time at Unilever and Bharti-Walmart. So performance and execution weren't the issue.

The problem was that the math didn't work for Snapdeal to own its own logistics company. In fact, it was far worse than that. As our research concluded, if Snapdeal didn't unload Vulcan Express it would, over time, bring down the e-commerce company altogether.

A big part of the problem lies with the logistics space in general. It's an extremely expensive and labour-intensive sector. You have to be able to box, ship, and deliver packages across a vast service region or, in the case of international business, all across the planet. Vulcan Express had some 15 warehouses and 166 hubs totalling just under 900,000 sq. ft of space that sprawled across 100 cities and 2,000 pin codes.

Not only did this require an army of delivery workers, it also meant you had to have down-to-the-second digital tracking systems that could tell a customer at any second of the day where their parcel was and when it would be delivered. In Snapdeal's heyday, the company could bleed cash from logistics costs and not feel the pain. But the music stops at some point.

Now, there are large logistics companies in India. But to manage it all as your *own company* can be a nightmare. Why? In two words, 'extra capacity'. If purchases on your primary e-commerce business go down, you end up getting stuck with a lot of extra capacity that will kill you. Put simply, if Snapdeal's e-commerce purchases on the website dipped for a couple months, Vulcan Express would be sitting around with tons of employees and overheads and not enough packages to process and deliver to pay for it all.

Better to let another logistics company worry about such things and contract with a vendor to avoid all the headaches and costs.

Despite all this, I knew the decision to divest of Vulcan Express was going to be controversial. Rohit was passionate about the business. He said he thought it could work and that we should keep it. I did my best to persuade him that the costs were going to kill us. I pointed out that e-commerce companies throughout the world that depend on their own end-to-end logistics business have not been profitable. Still, he was committed to figuring out a way to salvage Vulcan Express. I was pessimistic about the odds, but admired his determination to try to devise a solution. Wisely, Rohit agreed I should plan ahead and develop contingencies to sell it if efforts to fix Vulcan Express were unsuccessful.

But as time went by, the losses kept piling up. Worse, they were often growing larger and larger with each passing month. The logistics costs were a gaping and ever-widening hole that was going to suck Snapdeal down into the depths.

There were many reasons to sell Vulcan versus restructuring or shutting it down entirely. First, restructuring it or shutting it down would have required an investment of tens of millions of dollars. That was money we didn't have. Second, if we tried to sell it, we might make a little money in the sale, and this cash would build on the gains from our FreeCharge sale. Third, if we sold it, we could help the company's employees keep their jobs. Finally, a lot of Snapdeal's business already went through Vulcan Express so shutting it down would trigger service interruptions and upset our core e-commerce business. It was clear that selling the logistics company was the best way to go. Rohit agreed and gave me the green light to try and sell it.

And then … we got a big bucket of cold business reality splashed in our faces.

When we went to market, the general response was, 'Yeah, no. We don't want your logistics company at any price!'

Vulcan Express was running out of money. The scale had plunged. And nearly 100 per cent of its revenues came from Snapdeal—a company still in turmoil and battling for survival. None of these facts worked in our favour. It was clear we were going to have to work extremely hard to sell a company that was not likely to generate much cash. Put simply, we were going to have to work a lot to make very little.

One of the things I did to improve efficiency during deal-making was to hire a Big Four (KPMG, Deloitte & Touche, PricewaterhouseCoopers, Ernst & Young) company to analyse the business we were selling and to create a comprehensive financial report, also known as Vendor Due Diligence (VDD). This would point out red flags that we could resolve before finding a buyer.

After completing their analysis, the firm would give you a letter certifying your report (which wasn't cheap) that you could give to interested parties. We did the same thing with renowned law firms—such as J. Sagar Associates and Trilegal—on the legal side called Legal Due Diligence (LDD); lawyers went through all the contracts to make sure there were no issues and created a comprehensive legal report that they certified.

I had these reports completed and ready to go before we took Vulcan Express to market. But when we finally got All-Cargo, an old-school Indian company, to express tepid interest in possibly buying Vulcan, they didn't want any part of our Big Four report. They said they did their work the old-fashioned way from scratch. That set in motion a longer, inefficient process. (On the upside, I ended up becoming friends with the founder.)

As things dragged on, the terms kept changing. 'Sorry, we have to drop the price,' they said. 'We can't get our head around the numbers.' With no other buyers, we didn't have many options. So, we kept the deal going.

Then with a 100-page deal hammered out, we were on the verge of closing.

'Have your board ready and on standby,' they instructed. 'The call should be coming in two hours.'

The two hours came and went. Then two weeks came and went. Finally, out of nowhere, they called everything off. No deal. They no longer wanted to buy Vulcan Express.

Enter Future Group, founded by Kishore Biyani. They had a logistics company they were about to take public (Future Supply Chain) and were interested in snapping up Vulcan quickly. In exactly three days (Friday to Monday), we crafted a fully negotiated 100-page agreement for a $6 million sale. The deal was done and signed. But then something happened. Future Group said they couldn't close by December, due to some regulatory restrictions.

Then another road block popped up. Someone had filed a frivolous lawsuit for $50 million against Snapdeal and Vulcan, in an apparent effort to try to block the sale of Vulcan Express.

'This is the never-ending deal!' I told Kunal. 'This deal is cursed!'

I went back to Future Group and they said, 'We're paying $6 million for a company with a $50 million claim against it?!'

I had to come up with a way to give Future Group assurance that the lawsuit and surrounding media hype from it were nonsense. So we sent them all the documents and agreed to indemnify them.

January 2018 rolled around. Future Group went silent. They weren't responding to emails on closing actions. I called Kishore's office. It seemed someone had put the brakes on the deal and I didn't know why.

Then, two days later, Future Group resurfaced and said sorry for the delay, we're still closing the deal.

'No one is popping champagne bottles,' I told my guys. 'Not even when the paperwork is signed. A deal isn't done until the wire hits.'

A deal isn't done until the wire (money transfer) hits (your bank account)—those were words of wisdom I'd carried with me since I'd first learned them from my Wharton professor Eric Siegel. They have served me well along my entrepreneurial journey in tempering expectations and rebounding from disappointment when, inevitably, a deal falls through.

Life in business can change for bad or good in a nanosecond. There is that split-second—a sliver of time—right before a person signs a deal wherein they instantly go from middle class to exceedingly wealthy. Likewise, there is that same millisecond moment when a person goes from riches to rags and loses it all. Bottom line—don't assume a deal is done just because papers have been signed. And by all means, do not under any circumstances go out and spend money celebrating a deal whose funds have yet to transfer.

Thankfully, in the case of Snapdeal's sale of Vulcan Express to Future Group, the wire did hit. In the end we sold Vulcan Express for $6 million. Snapdeal management had been investing approximately 50 per cent of their time and bandwidth on Vulcan, while the value was less than one per cent of the main business. This was possibly even more detrimental than the financial losses. It was hard to let go of the company, but it was the only way forward.

As Kunal later explained, 'In January 2018, we were successful in finding a good home with the Future Group for our logistics company, Vulcan Express. This brought us closer to our aim of focusing exclusively on the marketplace. In hindsight, I would say that we used to spend much more time on solving logistics-related issues than solving for building a robust marketplace, our primary business.'

He added, 'While one could argue that owning a captive logistics setup was table stakes in light of the competitive dynamics, in hindsight it is clear that opening new fronts of a business adds complexity in geometric progression with an inevitable dilution of focus.'

As for the FreeCharge and Vulcan employees themselves, I wanted to do something to safeguard them from leaving after the Snapdeal restructuring. So I created a unique and generous retention plan to keep the most important assets of each company—the employees—in place and protected. The payments were in part a 'thank you' for the hard work they had put into building their respective businesses. It wasn't their fault what happened at Snapdeal. I wanted to share a portion of each sale's proceeds with the employees who made it possible. Some investors disagreed with me, but I felt strongly that this was both the right thing to do and good for business.

The bonus payout over a period of six-to-twelve months would help ensure that employees stayed before, during, and after the sales. That meant a win-win for the seller, the buyer, and the employees. It would also help ensure that the buyer was not left empty-handed and give the buyer the feeling that they were treated fairly by Snapdeal—a longer term business view.

I also baked in a provision to insulate the employees from any downside by making sure that if the buyer decided to lay off employees before the six to twelve-month payment time period, the employees would then receive a balloon payment (that is, the entire bonus and pay they were promised if they stayed with the company). My goal was to create an insurance policy of sorts to protect them and provide peace of mind and security. Besides, they deserved the life-changing bonuses. It was a critical factor in us successfully selling FreeCharge and Vulcan.

As I often tell my team members, the goal is to get the best possible outcome—not a perfect outcome—but the best outcome one can manage given the circumstances. By that measure, we were able to place Vulcan Express and its employees in strong and capable hands with Future Group. And we navigated around the financial iceberg directly in Snapdeal's pathway so we could keep the ship afloat and optimise the core e-commerce business.

Helping others often generates more joy, than just helping yourself. This is one of my greatest learnings to date. That was my experience with the Snapdeal turnaround. Kunal and Rohit had lived the ultimate entrepreneurial dream. Ten years prior, working out of a home basement in Delhi, they'd started a coupon book company. That start-up soon morphed into Snapdeal, a $6.5 billion e-commerce behemoth that jockeyed for position with the likes of Flipkart and Amazon.

Then, after a near-cataclysmic collapse, the company hunkered down, fought back, and came out winning. Kunal and Rohit deserve every good thing that comes their way; they've more than earned it. And they did it with teamwork, execution, determination, and bravery—core values that define champions.

From the near-fatal ashes of defeat, Snapdeal went from a ₹150 crore monthly loss business to cash flow positive, the first for an Indian consumer e-commerce company.

Instead of just a few months of runway left, Snapdeal had an indefinite runway with ₹1,000 crore in the bank. Despite a decline in GMV, net revenues went up. In other words, Snapdeal no longer required money from anyone else and was able to stay independent and take control of its own destiny—just as the founders wanted.

That's the ultimate win for mature entrepreneurs: a profitable and growing business that you control, not endlessly raising more and more investor money.

11

Resilience Is Essential

WHEN OFFERING ADVICE to entrepreneurs I'd always maintained that there is a right way and a wrong way to exit a company. Strive to leave on mutually beneficial and positive terms, I advised. Be in constant communication with your partners. And adopt an 'other-orientation' when discussing why it might be in both parties' interests to complete your chapter together and turn the page.

Now it was time to heed my own advice. I'd been thinking about it for a while. It was time to have 'the talk' with Kunal.

'After I finish up work on this last divestment, I don't know if there's much more for me to do that makes it worth you having me stay,' I said.

'Well, maybe we should have that conversation,' Kunal replied.

'I'm focused on getting this final deal done; it's important for the company. But I feel that I've done all the things I wanted to do here at Snapdeal,' I said.

Devising the Snapdeal 2.0 strategy and plan, helping restructure, selling off the companies that were weighing down the Snapdeal ship—the work and results had all been deeply rewarding. But I knew Kunal and Rohit could find someone at less cost to handle the lighter work that remained. I didn't know whether it made sense to keep me if Snapdeal was voyaging into calmer waters.

'I don't know what more there is for me to do that you really need me for versus getting someone else,' I said. 'Does it make sense for the company to keep rewarding me at this high level if there's nothing big for me to do? I'm just trying to look at this from your perspective.'

I framed the discussion this way because I believe it's important that exit conversations begin not solely from your vantage point, but also from the perspective of what's in the company's best interests. Then, once you've conveyed your respect and consideration for the other side, it's appropriate to pivot to your own concerns.

'Kunal, you know I'm used to being the CEO. It's where I'm most comfortable and happy. But if you really need me you know I'll stay and help with whatever needs to get done,' I said.

His face let me know he was a little sad to hear I was considering leaving, but he recognized I had a point.

'What about your team? They are really good guys. We could fit them in, but they don't naturally have obvious roles.'

Kunal's consideration for the well-being of my team meant the world to me. I appreciated the expression of concern.

'You're right,' I said. 'They don't have much left to do after we wrap up the deal I'm working on. I know them. Beyond getting a paycheck, they're not going to be fulfilled unless they're working at full capacity as well. But I really appreciate you asking about them.

Don't worry. I will take care of them wherever I go, or I'll find them positions.'

My decision to wind down my work for Snapdeal wasn't easy. I found the turnaround challenge fulfilling. I was also satisfied that we played a role in helping the founders gain greater legal control of their company while also giving the employees more upside and ownership in the business's future success.

Even though I didn't yet have a definite plan for my next move, I felt that old familiar interior tug—the inner gravitational pull that alerts me when it's time to work on building new assets inside myself.

Companies like Hotstar, WhatsApp India, Ola, Juul India, as well as a leading investment company, and a large government organization, among others, began approaching me for CEO or president roles. I decided to take a break to ensure that whatever I did next, I was passionate and energized about it. At the same time, I realized that one of the most valuable things a person can do to give back is to authentically share their journey and learnings to date, so I also decided to write this book.

I also decided that one of the personal growth skills I wanted to devote more time to involved serving as an effective and productive board member. A year prior I'd been approached by Dubai-based Emaar during their search for a new appointment to their board of directors for Emaar India.

One of the largest real estate developers in the world, Emaar, had already become a powerhouse in our country, with Indian assets valued at over $2 billion, over 3,000 acres of land, and over 10,000 people. At one point, Emaar was going to go public in India at a $10 billion valuation. Given my work as Housing.

com CEO, I had apparently blipped Emaar's radar screen in their search for a board member. Still, I was in my thirties; it was my understanding they were looking for an older, more senior candidate. Nevertheless, the executive-search firm leading Emaar's board-recruitment process said they would be in touch about setting up an interview.

I found the whole thing intriguing. Several years prior I'd taken my first trip to Dubai. While there, I saw many beautiful Emaar buildings, including the Burj Khalifa, the tallest building in the world, as well as the Dubai Mall, the world's largest mall. As I peered up at the glimmering Burj Khalifa, I distinctly remember thinking to myself, *I hope one day I can afford to be an Emaar customer and buy an Emaar apartment.* But at the time the idea seemed far-fetched, an entrepreneurial dreamscape.

Now, only a few years later, Emaar was calling about a possible appointment to its board of directors. After multiple interviews, I was finally interviewed by the board chairman and Emaar Group founder, His Excellency Mohamed Alabbar, one of the most successful and influential business leaders in the Middle East. I found him to be grounded, passionate, intellectually curious, and extremely smart. He also had an inspiring charisma that put you at ease. For example, my age was sort of the elephant in the room. So he addressed it with a gentlemanly smile and said, 'You know, I was actually your age when I founded Emaar.'

Shortly after the interviews were complete, I was appointed to the board of directors of Emaar India. As fate would have it, Emaar was undergoing a turnaround process, complete with a new business plan, management team, and restructuring—familiar ground for me. But service on the Emaar board also provided a personal growth opportunity to learn more about how a renowned international real estate developer operates. That excited me. It was a chance to develop *myself* as an asset, not just my financial assets.

I also became a senior advisor to the founder and CEO of a publicly listed technology company. In this role, I focused on creating the strategy for the next phase of growth and revamping investor relations. This gave me the opportunity to not only make a difference to the over ten-year-old company, but also learn first-hand about B2B software businesses and the process of managing a public company, which, in turn, further added to my skills and learnings.

This is an important point for entrepreneurs. While board and advisory positions often do not have major financial benefits, they offer vital opportunities to increase your experience, capabilities, and relationships—which in turn increases the value of yourself as an asset. Never accept a board appointment lightly. They typically require significant investments of your time and focus. Also, depending on the type of board you join, they may also involve fiduciary responsibilities with legal implications. Yet the chance to grow your abilities and contribute value as part of a board of directors is richly rewarding.

Board service can also spark exciting opportunities. As in the case of Emaar, Mr Alabbar had founded a Middle East e-commerce company called Noon.com with the vision of making it a sector leader in the region. Before its launch, Noon.com had raised $1 billion from Mr Alabbar and the Saudi Arabia's Public Investment Fund (the same investor behind Masa's Softbank Vision Fund)—the highest ever for a Middle East tech start-up. Later, Noon.com formed a five-person senior advisory group. Mr Alabbar asked me to join him after working together on the Emaar India Board.

One of the critical tasks before our group was deciding whether Noon.com should buy Souq.com—the Middle East's largest e-commerce company at the time. My colleagues and I dug in, performed a 360-degree analysis of Souq.com, and recommended Noon.com should buy it from a competitive strategy standpoint.

We counselled that if Amazon.com bought Souq with their strong capital base, it could create a competitive roadblock for Noon.com. Our group recommended Noon should buy Souq for between $800 million and $1 billion.

But then, just days later, Amazon bid for Souq! Noon countered at a higher price. And then ... silence. Souq didn't respond to Noon, because it had already agreed to exclusive discussions with Jeff Bezos's Amazon. The writing was on the wall. Amazon bought Souq. The landscape for Noon was about to shift. And fast.

Meetings were called to create a new strategy for Noon. I took day trips to Dubai from Delhi for meetings. We needed to devise a plan for Noon to compete against Amazon in the Middle East market. Noon was operating in a very different market than the Indian e-commerce environment Snapdeal had to navigate through.

Indeed, strategy is always dependent on the specific context in which a business operates, including the market you're in, where your company stands in that market, and your business's capabilities, resources, and goals. Also, strategy should be re-evaluated regularly; it can morph and evolve over time as circumstances change.

Noon's capabilities and access to resources, for example, were much greater than those we had to work with at Snapdeal. So, while the Noon strategy was quite different, the result was a successful e-commerce launch. Throughout, Mr Alabbar was open-minded towards the best ideas, humble, and thankful for others' efforts. His passion and humility inspired you to give your best to the group and its mission.

Along your entrepreneurial journey you will likely have chances to serve on boards or advisory committees. If the companies and executives involved align with your values and provide rapid learning or growth in areas that excite you, seize these opportunities. Doing so will cultivate intangible qualities within you. These personal assets often yield dividends that far exceed whatever financial remuneration you may give up in time devoted to board service. In addition, being in fellowship with other board directors will foster meaningful friendships that will provide insight and encouragement as you fight the good fight in pursuit of your entrepreneurial aspirations and goals.

Well, there you have it—one entrepreneur's journey from rebellious kid to CEO and beyond.

Looking back over the course of my business career to date, many common denominators and lessons emerge. In preparation for writing this book I spent considerable time thinking and distilling these learnings and takeaways down. My goal throughout has been to help you on your entrepreneurial journey by sharing things I wish others had shared with me.

If I had to boil it all down to a single theme it would be that businesses that fail or suffer serious turmoil often lack well-researched strategy and business models for sustainable growth and profitability. If you don't have a clear blueprint, the structure you build is bound to have flaws. Conversely, if you set your business up the right way from the start, you can avoid many dangers and defects.

Let me go one step further. I want to give you something that took me years to develop, streamline, simplify, and refine—my business model blueprint for the ideal start-up.

First, a little background. I'm often asked to give talks to entrepreneurs and businesses about the best way to build an upstart that attracts venture capital investment. Through the years I began condensing down the mountains of research data and analyses I and my team have performed on our businesses as well as our competitors throughout the world. At first, I just kept mental notes. But then I realized a larger, more comprehensive picture was beginning to take shape. So I jotted down snippets of data points and patterns.

Then several years ago my alma mater asked me to serve as a Wharton business plan competition judge. I remembered how valuable the feedback I'd received during the SprayIt entrepreneur competition was for me. I wanted to help pass the torch. So, in the many years I've served as a judge, I developed a rubric to assess the strengths and weaknesses of business plans from some of the best and brightest young minds—men and women who will go on to become the next generation of business leaders.

Doing so forced me to chisel all my learnings and knowledge down, smoothen the rough edges, and create a clear and polished framework. The result: seven golden pillars of the ideal start-up.

Before I give these to you, two caveats. First, following these seven steps will not guarantee that your entrepreneurial vision will be a success. There's no such thing as a bulletproof business plan. But understanding and following the seven golden pillars will dramatically increase the odds that you will develop an idea worthy of investor consideration. Indeed, as an angel investor myself, any time I consider making a personal capital investment in a company, I use these exact seven metrics to determine whether I want to invest.

Second, it is rare for an entrepreneur to have all seven pillars firmly in place at the outset. But if your start-up meets most of these, you are very likely going to attract funding. Why? Because hardwired into this framework's architecture are the traits most investors seek in a potential homerun winning company or idea. Also, if you have core pillars in place, it will prove extremely helpful when you create your business strategy.

Here, then, in no particular order, are my seven golden pillars for an ideal start-up:

1. Large and Growing Market Size
2. High Margin
3. Scalable
4. Proven Management Team
5. Less Capital Intensive
6. Sustainable Competitive Advantage
7. Established Business Model

This is the framework for the *ideal* start-up. Hardly ever does a start-up meet all these criteria, but it can be helpful to keep these in mind when refining a start-up idea or considering an early stage investment in an area of interest. Most importantly, though: don't forget your passion and gut!

On the surface, the seven pillars appear simple. But they contain distilled insights. Let me briefly highlight some of the finer points of each pillar.

1. *Large and Growing Market Size:* Many brilliant entrepreneurs with compelling business ideas don't attract resources because they are solving small problems that have niche markets. The point here is even if you do everything right and 'win', the impact and rewards are still limited. But the years of time required, hard work, sacrifice, and requisite risks are often similar to tackling larger problems. So the ideal start-up focuses on bigger problems and markets knowing that even if they're moderately successful, it's still likely to create a larger and more impactful company. Also, a growing market can be important long term because a rising tide lifts all ships. On the other hand, the vice versa is also true and going against the tide can create dangerous dynamics as when markets contract, players aggressively fight for turf and survival.

2. *High Margin:* A high-margin business can be seen as one with high unit economics. If you can consistently make a large profit per sale of your product or service, then naturally your business as an aggregation of many sales will have a relatively short and clear path to making profits and, eventually, large profits. Low-margin businesses require large scale to turn a business profitable and give you less margin of error to operate, which creates more risk.

3. *Scalable:* A scalable business allows you to increase sales rapidly and at low cost and is a golden combination with high-margin businesses. Many technology companies are high gross margin and scalable businesses—as a result, they have created massive value relative to the capital they required and therefore the space continues to attract enormous investment.

4. *Proven Management Team:* A proven management team is one that has done it before—maybe not exactly the same thing but as close to it as possible (and ideally together). This can dramatically reduce the execution risk. Business is a vast ocean and almost none of it is inherent knowledge; it's learning by experience. So relevant experience can vastly change a business plan from being pure theory to a high-probability reality. Investors of course know this and often place significant value on a team's prior experience.

5. *Less Capital Intensive:* A business that's very capital intensive can dilute entrepreneurs' and investors' ownership (and control) significantly over time and requires a higher return to justify the higher capital requirement. A lot of investors prefer to stay away from these kinds of businesses, and they can become particularly challenging during economic downturns when capital is scarce.

6. *Sustainable Competitive Advantage:* If a company is launched and is successful, it often motivates others to start similar competing businesses. Thinking ahead and understanding how you will sustain against this potential competition if you're initially successful is important, as it can determine the difference between a flash-in-the pan success and a business of enduring value.

7. *Established Business Model:* Drawing on established business models can be critical in the probability of success of a venture. Creating new businesses and products or services is itself risky, so layering on top of that a novel business model further multiplies the risk. Of course, this is required sometimes if it's something truly disruptive, but then it should be clear to all involved that it is high risk. Often, the belief is that at least 80 per cent of a business model should be drawn from what's occurred before in your market and industry (or other similar markets and industries). There shouldn't be more than 20 per cent business-model innovation. A long and rich history of successful and unsuccessful companies exists, so try and maximize your learnings from this. History does repeat itself in different shapes and forms.

This thought matrix is meant to ensure that you keep the important elements of business in clear view as you ideate and iterate your business concepts. Again, this is the exact framework I use as an angel investor or CEO when systematically analysing the health and viability of companies.

Now that you have the business blueprint, before you set off on your journey, I want to impress upon you four mental concepts that will help optimize your entrepreneurial mindset.

1. **Balance:** A principle that runs deep even in nature. Take food. We know that eating too much of one thing isn't good for you. This applies even to some of the healthiest food, such as superfoods. Similarly, we're told to stay well hydrated by drinking plenty of water. That is absolutely true. Most of us, if we admit it, don't drink enough. But drinking too much water too fast is bad for you. Doctors have a name for it: hyponatremia, also known more commonly as water intoxication.

   In fact, in extremely rare cases, guzzling down gallons of water fast can even lead to death from the dilution of sodium levels in your blood. The point is not that we shouldn't eat healthy or drink enough water; rather, that even the healthiest of behaviours can turn dangerous without proper balance.

   Now I know what you're thinking: *Jason, I thought you were the guy who always liked to push things to extremes? 1,000 pushups a day, playing education audio tapes while you sleep to try to learn more, treks to Muay Thai kickboxing camps in Thailand to train—and now you're telling me that 'balance' is important?!* I get it. I do. But hear me out. Saying that balance is important does not diminish the importance of intensity. Quite the contrary. It means eliminating the unnecessary or unhealthy things you spend time on and refocusing that energy and intensity on things that are positive and beneficial. Moreover, I have discovered that most of the limits of what we think are possible are actually self-imposed mental barriers; humans can do much more than we've been led to believe.

   As the saying goes, the problem isn't that most people aim too high and miss; the problem is that most people aim too low and hit. But balance applies to everything. For example, being thoughtful is always important, but overthinking can confuse someone just as much as not thinking much at all. We are often conditioned to think in a simple way that says certain things are good and we should have as much of them as possible, while other things are bad and we should have as little of them as possible. But that's lazy logic. Malcolm Gladwell makes this point. It's like looking at a line graph that spikes when you have more of something, plateaus and levels off when you gain even more of it, and then plunges once you reach the tipping point of excess.

Now apply this principle to money. I am consistently reminded of the illusions and myths surrounding wealth. Balance is critical when learning how to manage your finances as they grow throughout your entrepreneurial journey. This also extends to the way it will affect future generations of your family. For example, I know people who inherited so much money that their life's responsibility is to protect their wealth by diversifying it, investing it prudently, and ensuring that they maximize tax efficiency, including where they live and for how long.

For these individuals the money accumulated is so vast that it simply does not make financial sense for them to do anything else in life but focus on these objectives even when there are many things in life that would bring them greater fulfilment, satisfaction, and joy. For example, they may really want to live in a certain country, but tax-wise it would cost them millions of dollars extra, so they cannot bring themselves to move.

Should we feel sorry for these poor millionaires and billionaires trapped in their platinum palaces? No, that's not what I'm saying (nor what most of them would suggest either). But the principle is that even something that seems like a great problem to have—massive riches—can devolve into something less than great. If you doubt this, just look at the sad and tragic examples of the lives of the rich and famous who, despite having fame and fortune, turned tragic through self-destructive or decadent behaviour.

Bottom line: maintaining proper balance is vital for a healthy business. You can't build a solid business only looking at one parameter; you must adopt a multi-dimensional view. That's just as true for living a healthy life as it is for building a thriving business.

2. **Cycles:** The second mindset principle is to realize that everything goes in cycles. That is the way of the world. What goes up will come down and vice versa. Nothing lasts forever. This is true of countries, markets, industries, and life itself.

   Cycles are a result of a confluence of many factors and cannot be changed. But you can decide what you will do in each stage of the cycle. For example, businesses that raise capital during a boom time and conserve this capital until a down time often outlast and outmanoeuvre competition by being able to invest in growth and acquisition when others cannot, versus doing so when many others can too. The same is true for the hardships of life. We can't control serious illness or the loss of a loved one. But by cultivating spiritual and mental growth, we can strengthen our hearts and minds to traverse the hardships life brings and still find contentment, peace, and joy.

3. **Categorize:** The third mindset concept that will serve you well is quite simple but useful: realize that there are a number of categories in life—and that not everything you're passionate about should be a business you start. This is important. People often hear leaders say 'do what you're passionate about' and misinterpret that to mean they should

launch new business ventures based solely on the things that excite them. That's misguided.

A better way to organize your entrepreneurial thoughts is to sort things into categories in your life. Think of these as four separate buckets. One of these buckets we might label 'things I only consume', such as South Indian food. I happen to love this cuisine, but just because I enjoy it does not mean I should run out and launch a South Indian restaurant.

A second bucket would be 'things I consume or enjoy casually learning about', such as Thai boxing. Did I drop out of Wharton and pursue a career or business based on a causal interest in the sport? No. Thai boxing belonged in the second category of things I like to learn about for enjoyment, not upend my life and career path over.

Third, there are 'hobbies or interests that require part-time involvement'. For me, this tends to be things like creative endeavours such as movie projects or books like this one. This third bucket is reserved for things you're passionate about enough to devote energy and focus to for a limited and defined period of time, but not something that requires you to restructure your entire life or career long-term.

Fourth and finally, there is that most serious bucket of all—the one labelled 'full-time or lifelong commitments'. This category holds the most important implications. For example, entrepreneurship and spiritual development are two of the things in this category for me personally. Everyone is different. The point is that by using the mental tool of thinking of life in categories, we can remain thoughtful in prioritizing what truly matters and deserves our greatest time and focus.

4. **Resilience:** Finally, if you remember nothing else from this chapter remember this: resilience is essential. (I even made that the chapter title to pound home the point). Throughout my story you've seen me when I was in the doldrums and wanted to quit … but kept lumbering forward anyway.

   People thought I was crazy to buy Valiant, and even crazier to stick with it when it looked bleak and hopeless. When I accepted the CEO position for Housing.com, some cautioned I might be committing career suicide. I bet otherwise. And when I took on Snapdeal and FreeCharge, I'm sure to outside observers my decision to step into companies in peril seemed irrational. I pressed ahead. I say these things to encourage you.

   Do not lose heart.

   Believe in yourself.

   Follow your passion.

   Have confidence in your abilities.

   Have faith in your vision.

   Remain humble.

   Never quit.

   Resilience is essential.

   Pursue your dreams secure in the knowledge that the history of entrepreneurship is replete with the stories of those who failed over and over only to achieve success later as they learned and iterated through setbacks. Let me be crystal clear: some days you're absolutely going to want to quit. You will ask yourself what's the point of carrying on. Naysayers' voices will crowd your mind. *Maybe they're right*, you'll think to yourself. *Maybe I'm not cut out for the entrepreneurial life.* Ignore the doubters. Push past the self-defeating thoughts. Realize you are not alone in feeling these things. Everyone who has made it in business has been right where you are.

The difference between winning and losing is the will to march forward when others quit or fall to the wayside.

Few things strengthen the trait of resilience like failure. As legendary Bollywood producer and media mogul Ronnie Screwvala put it: 'Failure fascinates and intrigues me. I've never understood why people are so afraid to fail … Failure is a part of life. Everyone fails. I know I have. More times than I can count. I am routinely asked questions about my various entrepreneurial experiences, and most want to hear about the successes. Why don't they ask about the failures? It would give me more to talk about.'

Now, the reason I gave you the seven core pillars of an ideal start-up is because mastering those principles early in your entrepreneurial lifecycle can help minimize the frictions and setbacks that will tempt you to quit in the first place. That said, even with the seven pillars of an ideal start-up firmly in place, you're still going to have to fight like hell. Doing so will condition your body, mind, and spirit to assume larger responsibilities, sharpen your personal assets and skills, and expand and scale your vision to greater heights. Learn to enjoy the struggle. Wear your battle scars as the badges of honour that they are. Just like the Thai kickboxing Fighter of the Century, Apidej Sit Hirun, said to me: smile when you're getting punched and keep fighting.

None of this is easy. All of it is worth it.

Joining the tribe of entrepreneurship isn't for everyone. It's a rare breed who is willing to live and work on his or her own terms and give up the illusion of safety and security that comes from following the dictates of society. But in my opinion, the rewards far outweigh the risks. Achieving personal and financial freedom, being your own boss, creating value and opportunities for others, doing work you're passionate about and believe in—dreaming up your own business idea, bringing it to fruition, and living the entrepreneurial life can be an exhilarating adventure.

So stop waiting for the planets to align and sprinkle your dreams down from the heavens. It won't happen. Nothing works if you don't.

If a rebellious, rootless kid can go from bare-knuckle brawls and alcohol-fuelled hospital emergencies, to CEO and one of the top ten most highly paid executives in the country, imagine what you can do.

You've got this. Get moving.

Everything is possible.

Turn it around.

Epilogue

IF YOU'VE MADE it this far into this book, you've seen me at my worst and my best, personally and professionally. The process of entrepreneurial maturation is sometimes painful and fraught with embarrassing, head-smacking mistakes that make you cringe if you ponder them too long. That's true of life in general, though, isn't it?

Upon deeper reflection, however, you realize that all the pieces of your journey fit together. Indeed, once you pull back at panoramic and trace the flight path of your life, something amazing—magical even—happens. Like a time-lapse video of a portrait being painted in hyper-speed, the brush strokes of life—the joys, tears, mistakes, victories—all swirl seamlessly into a masterpiece bursting with colour and meaning. Not perfection, but insight. Not flawlessness, but authenticity. It's your story. There are no others like it. It's yours and yours alone.

Life is messy. So is business.

The question is: how can you make the greatest impact for your family and others amid the mess? One way to unlock the answer to that riddle is by reflecting on the places where your spirit draws inspiration. I am inspired by people who set bold goals and overcome significant obstacles to achieve them. I am in awe of people who do this at an exceptional level in their daily lives. It makes the seemingly complex challenges of turning around and building companies appear small and solvable by comparison.

The single mother who gets up before sunrise each morning and works two jobs to provide for her children; the father who sacrifices material comforts to save funds so his children can go to college and live a better life; the young cancer patient who smiles through the pain with a grateful heart that longs to live and love—nothing in business will ever compare to the heroism found in the souls of ordinary people living extraordinary lives.

I've always been drawn to the indomitable nature of the human spirit. I suppose that's why I was so entranced with comics as a child. For me it's always been about understanding and studying that thing inside a person that says: 'I refuse to give in. I will not quit. I choose to live. I choose to rise.' Whatever *that* was—I knew I wanted to capture that lighting in a bottle and let it illumine my path.

It's funny how your perception of what constitutes a 'great person' or 'great life' changes as you grow older, mature, and are exposed to different circumstances and ideas. When we're young, we often possess a surface view of success that's defined by things like athletics, popularity, or academics. Then, as we enter the early days of our careers, a 'great life' seems to be more a factor of money, authority, or fame. But once we hit that more evolved stage of life, we realize that making a difference in small and big ways in the lives of others is the path that leads to the most rewarding and lasting impact.

One historical figure who perhaps understood that better than almost anyone was Lord Mahavira, founder of modern Jainism and a Jain Tirthankara. He has long been a source of inspiration and encouragement for me. Mahavira was born as Vardharmana in 599 BCE in Bihar, during an era of spiritual disenchantment. Vardhamana's goal was as large and noble as it gets—to attain enlightenment or perfection and impart the resulting wisdom to better the world. However, his path was also as challenging as it gets—to give up all his personal attachments, including his family, and restrict sensory pleasures forever. He spent more than twelve years as a wandering monk, going through a process of refinement and meditation. Finally, in the thirteenth year of his penance, he reached enlightenment and transformed from Vardhamana to Mahavira ('Great Hero').

Today, there are five million Jains in the world who follow Mahavira. In addition, Siddhartha Gautama, a younger contemporary of Mahavira, was significantly influenced by his teachings. Siddhartha himself later reached enlightenment and became known as Buddha (meaning the Enlightened One). Buddhism has 500 million followers today.

In business or in life, when we discuss ambitious goals, complex challenges, sacrifices and large scale, I remind myself of Mahavira and a few others like him. He was a human being of flesh and blood, like you and me. Compared to him, our goals and challenges are miniscule and require us to barely scratch the surface of our potential. Everything is possible. I believe that. I hope you do, too.

A more contemporary historical source of inspiration for me is Walt Disney. If you study his story you realize that he overcame seemingly insurmountable obstacles to bring a vision others deemed insane to fruition. Beyond the massive business success his dream produced, Disney created a wholesome form of family entertainment that encouraged young dreamers to live their best life while instilling timeless virtues.

I keep a yellow Mickey Mouse figurine on my desk. Any time I'm feeling like there's a business challenge I can't solve, I look down at the small plastic statue and think of young Walt battling against the world to turn the whimsy and magic of childhood dreams into a corporate global empire that has brought smiles to the faces of children for generations in the form of theme parks and movies. Disney chose to master the worlds of animation and theme parks. What will your focus be?

There is a deeper satisfaction that can be achieved from mastering one's craft—one that has nothing to do with money or position. That's the great thing about being human: we all have the same number of hours in a day to work with in order to make something of ourselves. However, no one is better than anyone else. We are different but equal. Circumstances and choices drive outcomes.

In this book I've tried to convince you to consider the entrepreneurial path as a means towards personal development. The greatest value of entrepreneurship lies not in financial success but in the ways one's journey through business accelerates your personal evolution. For me, the journey generated happiness, peace, wisdom, and joy faster and earlier in my life than I would have otherwise experienced them. Why? Because business and life are not separate. Indeed, as I hope you've seen throughout this book, lots of personal life lessons can be applied in business situations and vice versa.

As much as I want you to at least consider entrepreneurship for your life, I do so with the full and complete understanding that the entrepreneurial lifestyle is not for everyone. Your tolerance for risk, problem-solving skills, level of passion, and most importantly, spirit of resilience must be strong. But if you're willing to get outside your comfort zone, take responsibility, and be resourceful, you will find that the entrepreneurial journey can be an adventure like no other.

Speaking of new and exciting adventures, I've been working on a film project for one of my other sources of inspiration—Bruce Lee—

whose iron will and determination seemed almost superhuman. Several years ago I bought the rights for Bruce Lee's final masterpiece, *The Silent Flute*. It is a philosophical martial arts epic about a raw fighter who overcomes trials to achieve enlightenment and become the best fighter in the world. Lee conceived the story but died before it could be produced. My old boss, Jackie Chan, idolized Bruce Lee. As a young stunt guy, Jackie had the privilege of working with Bruce Lee at the pinnacle of his success. As Jackie puts it, 'It was so nice to be hit by Bruce Lee!'

As funny as that quote is, it also contains a hidden truth: gratitude and learning can emerge even in adversity. It reminds me of one of my favourite Bruce Lee quotes: 'Do not pray for an easy life. Pray for the strength to endure a difficult one.' In my life, I have chosen entrepreneurship as the gauntlet through which to condition myself to overcome difficulties and refine my skills. In the military, they call the training facility used for testing material and equipment a 'proving ground'. I like that phrase. Business was the ground upon which I proved to myself that I was able to accomplish more than I thought possible.

Entrepreneurship can do that for you. It strengthens your inner eye—the ability to search inside yourself to improve weaknesses and polish talents. Leading people, studying the past to predict and strategize for the future, forming partnerships and doing deals, learning the intricacies of contracts and business laws, honing public and interpersonal communication skills, attracting and hiring talented people, management, marketing, mastering all the nuts and bolts of business—each of these challenges catapulted me forward. They forced me to improve, sharpen my skills, elevate, evolve. My hope for you is that you realize it's never too late to pursue your passion. It's never too late to turn it around.

Entrepreneurship won't make you better than other people, but it can make you a better version of yourself. It did, for me.

Index

Acknowledgements

Although in my 30s, a book about one's life experiences even up to this point still involves infinite thank you's – a person's life is a result of uncountable inputs and influences around them and mine is no different. I will only be able to cover a small fraction of thank you's here, so please forgive me if I don't call you out by name, it doesn't diminish your contribution nor the gratitude I have towards it.

Beginning with my family, thank you to my father and mother, brother Neil, sister-in-law Arthi, Anilkaka and Rakshakaki, Anjumasi, Bapuji and Ba, and Kaka and Ba, who have all indirectly or directly contributed significantly. Also, love to my nieces Saanvi and Naavya.

Thank you to all my mentors or advisors along the way, such as Vijay Parekh Uncle, Anirudh Patni, Akash Bhansali, Vallabh

Bhansali Uncle, Peter Dekom, Bill Jemas, Lawrence Gelburd, Bey Logan, Fred Armentrout, Shamus Mok, Lynn Franco, Matthew Anderson and Ken West, to name just a few, who have been very generous with their time and guidance. Also, the numerous virtual ones, whose autobiographies I have read and learned so much from, such as Andre Agassi, Richard Branson and Michael Caine, among many others.

Thank you to my book writing and publishing partners, including Wynton and Michelle Hall, who have been fantastic collaborators, and editor Sachin Sharma and CEO Ananth Padmanabhan at HarperCollins India, who have been supportive from day one. Thank you to Niraj Saraf, a colleague who has been an amazing partner and instrumental throughout the entire process. Thanks to Rohit Chawla, Siddharth Dasari, Aanchal Arora, Zeenat Khan, Sangram Surve, Rohan Shrestha, Nikhil Dey, Rohan Kanchan and Vishal Vincent, among others. Also, early reviewers Shefali Bhandari and Ashish Singodia, to name a few, who have helped me on the book.

Thank you to all the founders, teams and investors at Valiant Entertainment, Housing.com, FreeCharge and Snapdeal, who without their efforts, these companies would have ceased to exist. Business is a team sport, and the full list would be a whole book onto itself. Thank you also to my colleagues at Emaar.

Thank you to the valuable consultants along the way, such as Ken Henderson at Bryan Cave; Tim Pecsenye at Blank Rome; Scott Agostoni formerly at William Morris Endeavor; Eric Siegel at Wharton; Rohit Kale at Spencer Stuart; Jayendrabhai Shah at NA Shah; Nitish Poddar at KPMG; Harsh Pais at Trilegal; Siddharth Shankar at J. Sagar & Associates; Haigreve Khaitan and Siddharth Shah at Khaitan & Co.; and their respective teams, among others.

Thank you to friends, such as Chris Gadbury, Tony Mehta, Glynda Alves, Mukul Deora and Nitasha Thapar, Kunal and Yashna Bahl, Suvir Sujan, Vishal Mehta, Sarah Williams, Samarth and Niyati

Parekh, Minoru, Jamshid Pandole, Sid Talwar, among many others. Also, thank you to all of YPO Mumbai Connect, especially my Mumbai 'family' – Apoorva Mehta, Sumit Jalan, Priti Gupta, Rakshit Desai, Vishal Gupta, Tushar Khanna and Shaishav Dharia – who are a steadfast support.

Thank you to the hardworking staff that assisted me since I moved to India, including my Mumbai driver Robert, my Delhi driver Pramod, the Grand Hyatt Mumbai staff, the Lodhi Hotel staff, and my various executive assistants Shikha, Leena, Lizia and Sakshi.

Thank you to the spiritual leaders that have been a source of inspiration, such as Lord Buddha, Lord Mahavira, and Shri Sai Baba.

Lastly, thank you to my detractors. When you're a turnaround man, it's impossible to do so without some people disliking you, no matter how fair and good you try to be. Any changes, even big positive ones, involve boosting some people's situation but also displacing others. My detractors have helped me avoid complacency and pushed me to forge new paths and make myself better. Without them, there wouldn't be 'me', so keep it coming and thank you ☺.

About the Author

Jason Kothari is a passionate entrepreneur and business turnaround leader.

While still in college, he acquired the bankrupt US-based Valiant Entertainment for less than a million dollars. He then led the transformation of the company as the CEO to the third largest superhero entertainment company after Marvel and DC Comics and a sale for $100 million, a record industry return. The Company was named *Publisher of the Year*, was nominated for 90 awards, and completed a landmark five-movie deal with Sony Pictures based on its characters. This includes *Bloodshot* (2020) starring Vin Diesel, where Jason served as an Executive Producer.

Subsequently, Jason was the CEO of Housing.com, one of India's largest online real estate companies, where he led the transformation of the distressed company and then a merger with News Corp's

PropTiger to create the $350 million industry leader with News Corp, the largest strategic investor in the space globally, investing $50 million and becoming the lead investor. The Company had increased revenues by 400%, while reducing costs by 70%, and its platform became the most popular for buying and selling homes in the country.

Following this, Jason became the Chief Strategy & Investor Officer of Snapdeal, one of India's largest e-commerce companies valued at $6.5 billion at its peak, where he played a lead role in transforming the distressed company. This included leading the Snapdeal 2.0 strategy & plan creation, the restructuring of the company, and the sale of non-core businesses, resulting in the company going from an over $20 million monthly loss to a profit, a first for an Indian e-commerce company, and generating $140 million in excess cash.

During this time, Jason was also the CEO of FreeCharge, one of India's largest digital payments companies owned by Snapdeal, where he led the distressed company from a $10 million gross monthly loss a few months earlier to a gross profit and then a sale to Axis Bank for $60 million, a vital deal for Snapdeal's turnaround and a key strategic deal in the Indian fintech space.

In addition, he has been a senior advisor to various companies, such as Softbank, the largest technology investor; Noon.com, the largest e-commerce company in the Middle East that has raised $1 billion; Infibeam Avenues, the only publicly listed e-commerce company in India; and is on the Board of Directors of Emaar India, one of the largest real estate developers in India with over $2 billion in assets going through a turnaround.

He holds a B.S. from The Wharton School of the University of Pennsylvania and is a member of Young President's Organization (YPO).

He lives in Mumbai and is passionate about helping entrepreneurs and financing media projects about inspiring stories.